Diamonds Are A Dyke's Best Friend

D1002419

Diamonds Are A Dyke's Best Friend

reflections, reminiscences, and
reports from the field on the
lesbian national pastime

by
Yvonne
Zipter

Firebrand
Books
Ithaca, New York

This book may not be reproduced in whole or in part, except in the case of reviews, without permission from Firebrand Books, 141 The Commons, Ithaca, New York 14850.

Book and cover design by Mary A. Scott
Cover photographs by Marlene Serikaku
Typesetting by Bets Ltd.

Printed in the United States by McNaughton and Gunn

Cartoon Credits:
  Pages 61, 95, 112, 196-97: Alison Bechdel.
  Page 134: *And God Bless Uncle Harry and His Roommate Jack* (Avon, 1979).

Photograph Credits:
  Pages 53, 73, 91, 107, 131, 155, 177, and 191: Marlene Serikaku
  Page 27: *Winterthur Portfolio, A Journal of American Material Culture* (University of Chicago Press, Spring 1983).

Library of Congress Cataloging-in-Publication Data

Zipter, Yvonne, 1954–
    Diamonds are a dyke's best friend.

    Bibliography: p.
    1. Softball for women.   2. Lesbians—United
States—Recreation.   I. Title.
GV881.3.Z57   1988   796.357'8   88–30897
ISBN 0-932379-48-6
ISBN 0-932379-47-8 (pbk.)

This book is dedicated
to the Women and Children First softball team
and to my volleyball team, the Violent Femmes.

Acknowledgments

I don't know how many times I've looked at sections such as this and seen words like: "A book like this doesn't get written without the help of a lot of people." Now I know why.

I would like to thank the following:

Barbara Grier of the Lesbian and Gay Archives of the Naiad Press; the Lesbian Herstory Archives in New York; the Gerber-Hart Library in Chicago; the Women's Sports Foundation in New York; and the lesbian softball players from coast to coast who shared and entrusted me with their softball experiences;

Sharon Roepke for much of the information on the AAGPBL; Toni Armstrong and *Hot Wire*, in which part of Chapter 2 was previously published; all of my friends who distributed questionnaires and made other contacts for me; Helen Lenskyj for information on dyke softball in Canada; and Nancy K. Bereano, whose faith in me, along with her sharp editing skills, I am extremely grateful for, and without whom this book would not exist;

Val and Martha for financial assistance; and the Ragdale Foundation of Lake Forest, Illinois, where part of the work for this book was completed;

My coworkers at the University of Chicago Press for their support, enthusiasm, help, and, especially, their indulgence; Jan for helping me stay on schedule and for her ballplayer's critiques; Tracy Baim, my editor at *Outlines*, for giving me the space to hone my writing skills; the owners and staff of Women and Children First bookstore for answering a hundred questions, sponsoring readings of the book, and supporting my writing career for years now; Jorjet Harper for her editorial eye and general encouragement; Kathy Forde for help with typing and, even more important, the sound of her voice and a hug or a joke whenever I needed one; Linda Bubon for feeding me so often (literally and emotionally); Max Bubon (Linda's small son) for being a bright light in my life; and my sister Lori for being enthusiastic about everything I do.

Preface

Warming Up

At the 1986 National Women's Studies Association meeting, I told a friend I would be happy to give her a lift to the airport after the meeting, but I was hoping to do so in order to be back in time for my softball game. We began talking about the phenomenon of softball within the lesbian community, how dykes everywhere seem to play. Suddenly, my friend said to me, "Have you ever thought about doing a book on softball dykes?" I told her no and, what's more, though it sounded interesting, I didn't really have time to write a book. But later, back at my table in the exhibit hall, I found myself jotting down notes on what such a book would include, along with a title. Excited, I went to tell my friend what I had been thinking: "Well, *maybe* I can find the time. . . ." That friend was Nancy Bereano of Firebrand Books. And such was the genesis of *Diamonds Are A Dyke's Best Friend*.

Contents

Introduction

Touching All The Bases

Softball for me was a real statement. I came over from Hong Kong when I was seven and didn't speak any English. I remember this was one way I felt like I was proving myself to be an American. It was a really rough time because I was a real oddity in Iowa where my adoptive parents were. That's why I played sports. It was kind of an expression for me, a way of saying, "Hey, I'm an American—baseball is American." So I thought if I could play softball really well, baseball really well, I'd be accepted. (Mei)

To most lesbians, softball is more than just a game. It is a social event. It is a test of endurance and skill. It is the incubator for an extended family. It is a way of fitting in, of making friends. It is a statement of independence, of courage, of commitment. It is the sheer joy of outdoor physical activity. In short, it is the beauty of distinctly different parts coming together to form a whole; for some, it is almost a mystical experience.

Country dykes, city dykes, dykes with four-year degrees, dykes with no degrees, dykes who are feminists, dykes who aren't, dykes of different races and classes, dykes who have been athletes their whole lives, and dykes who are just discovering, or rediscovering after years, the values of athletic endeavors—there are softball players among all their ranks. Softball is one of the most universal and yet least examined aspects of our lesbian culture.

Diamonds Are A Dyke's Best Friend takes a step toward rectifying this oversight. It is a tribute to dyke softball, assessing its place and function in our community nationwide, why most of us love it (but some of us don't), its origins, foibles, and pitfalls. This tribute manifests itself in our songs, poems, cartoons, and personal stories and insights, a number of which are reprinted here. Though some of these observations and insights are from published sources, most are from women like myself—softball dykes from across the country who have shared their thoughts with me on questionnaires and in interviews. Some of what you read will be light-hearted, some will deal with more substantive issues. But all of it reflects the tremendous importance of softball in our lesbian subculture.

Writing this book was both a challenge and a pleasure. The challenge was twofold. First there was the task of finding other written materials on the subject of lesbians and softball. Several years later I can report that there *is* some—but not much. The other major challenge was to figure out a way—in the absence of prior research on the subject and with virtually no funds—to determine just what the place of softball is in lesbian communities across the country. Though it would never pass for scientific research, I was able to gather stories from coast to coast by sending a stack of questionnaires to every city where I knew someone—or where someone I knew knew someone —and asking them to hand them out to the softball dykes they knew. I also did several telephone interviews from the contacts I made through my expanded network of softball dykes.

But the pleasure I got from working on this book made tackling the challenges well worth it—pleasures like receiving questionnaires back in the mail, each filled with touching, entertaining, thought-provoking stories. Pleasures like hanging out at the softball field every weekend all summer long and telling myself, "It's research." Pleasures like discovering that women once played professional baseball and, even more exciting, getting to meet and spend time with many of the league's former players.

Diamonds Are A Dyke's Best Friend is of tremendous value for lesbians, particularly the softball dykes all across the country. The book is an act of pride, of courage, of vocally claiming what is rightfully ours—a place in the athletic world that we love. It's our way of thumbing our noses at the homophobic mist hovering silently over women's sports like a poisonous gas, our way of saying, "Yeah, some of us, the women who play sports, are lesbians—and we're proud of it."

Of course, not every woman is in a position to be safely out as a lesbian, and some stories are presented with pseudonyms. For those women (and thousands like them), this book is less a way of taking charge of our fate as lesbian athletes and more a source of validation. Generally, if we hear about lesbians in sports at all, it is in a derogatory manner, often distorting the importance that our sexuality plays in our approach to the game, to our teammates, to our coaches. *Diamonds Are A Dyke's Best Friend*, on the other hand, is a healthy—and more realistic—alternative, celebrating the lesbian athlete rather than stalking her like some terrible fugitive prey. Although this may sound melodramatic, lesbian witchhunts do happen in sports. Witness, for example, the one-man attack launched in 1986 by journalist Bill Figel in the *Chicago Sun-Times*.

SOFTBALL

An ode to our national pastime

Just about the same time every year
When the days get longer and the nights stay clear
Sneaks up like a thief and steals them all away
You can tell when they pull down the cleats
Can't sleep at night and refuse to eat
Everybody and her sister's getting ready to play

Softball, softball, the old ones hobble and the young ones crawl
For a big, strong woman it's the only game in town
Softball, softball, start in the springtime and swing till the fall
If you find a women's center and the staff is gone
I'll tell you where to find them and it won't take long
They're out there playing that old softball

The teams are run collectively till a bad-news umpire yells, "Strike 3"
And sometimes some of that sisterhood runs amok
But afterwards at the local bar, they debate at length who hit the
    farthest
And the losing team toasts the winners on their luck

Playing softball, softball, the old ones hobble and the young ones
    crawl
For a big, strong woman it's the only game in town
Softball, softball, start in the springtime swing till the fall
If you overhear an argument that's gone too far
It's over who left the bases in the back of the car
They're out there playing on the softball team.

In a series of three articles—almost a full page—Figel in-
itiated just such a lesbian witchhunt in women's professional and college athletics. He cites as reasons for fear
among young athletes (and their mothers), female coaches
who (he claims) exact sexual favors from their young
players. He also claims that athletes who are lesbians seek
to convert other young women to lesbianism. In fact, the
reverse is usually true: lesbians in sports are so fearful of

There's always one team tries to outdo all the rest
They arrive in identical lavender sweatsuits
Sweating identical lavender sweat
The team is made up of women that no one's ever seen
The rumor is they're the Yankees or a passing group from Queens

Playing softball, softball, the old ones hobble and the young ones
    crawl
For a big, strong woman it's the only game in town
Softball, softball, start in the springtime swing till the fall
If you can't pitch or field or hit to the fence
Put your consciousness back on the bench
They're out there playing that old softball

A big, strong woman I knew for years missed an easy bunt, was re-
    duced to tears
There's a whole new, brand new meaning for E.R.A.
Pop-up, short stop, one, two, three;
The basement team's in misery
But at the end of the season you can be sure they'll say
"Wait until next year. . ."

Softball, softball, the old ones hobble and the young ones crawl
For a big, strong woman it's the only game in town
Softball, softball, start in the springtime swing till the fall
I've heard it before but I'd like to amend
A baseball diamond is a girl's best friend
They're out there playing, out there giving their all
They're out there playing that old softball.

(From *Old Friends* by Judy Regan produced by Wild Patience Records, 1983.)

losing their jobs or jeopardizing their athletic careers that
they tend to be conservative and closeted. What makes
these articles by Figel most frightening is that there was
no apparent reason for them, no specific incident to which
they were related: Figel seems to have taken up this cause
personally of his own accord.[1]

Ignoring the topic of lesbians in sports, however—the
tack that many of us have taken until now—is clearly not

an effective way of dealing with things either. Keeping quiet about lesbian athletes is what feeds the fear, ignorance, and negative images that many harbor, and gives people like Figel the opportunity to go unchallenged. In addition, avoiding the topic of lesbianism prevents us from understanding all aspects of women and sports, including the prevalence of homophobia in the athletic community, our fears of being stigmatized, the need or desire to pass, and the place of sports—in this case, softball—in the lesbian community. Besides, "the presence of Lesbian girls and women is not the problem. Discrimination against them is the problem. As long as homophobia can be used to divide women, as long as heterosexual women are willing to disown and disparage Lesbians in an attempt to distance themselves from the costs and negative consequences of being considered Lesbian, men (and women) who feel threatened by strong women will be able to intimidate and inhibit *all* girls and women with a word."[2] On the other hand, when we claim the name *lesbian athlete* for ourselves, we take away some of that phrase's power as a threat against us.

Diamonds Are A Dyke's Best Friend is an honest, open look—an insider's look—at the special relationship between lesbians and softball, beginning, after a brief account of my personal softball history, with the placement of the lesbian-softball relationship in history. Have you ever stopped to think, for instance, why lesbians and *softball?* Why not lesbians and basketball? Or tennis? Or any of a number of other sports? Chapter 2, "From Out in Left Field: A Brief History," provides the historical context to answer such questions.

Chapter 3 discusses our early experiences with softball: who we learned to play from, who we played with, the ways we were encouraged athletically, and the ways we were discouraged. The next chapter, "Safe at Home: Softball as a Place of Refuge," is in some ways the heart of the book, as it explores the ways in which softball performs significant social functions in our nationwide lesbian community. And certainly *the* most social aspect of dyke softball involves teammates who are also lovers—the topic of Chapter 5, "The Double Play (Or, Love on the Softball Field)." The social nature of softball is without a doubt one of its biggest draws, but a variety of other factors make it appealing to us as well, including a wide range of purely physical sensations. The things we like to taste, smell, see, feel, and hear in connection with softball are the topics of Chapter 6, "The Pitch: The Aesthetics of Dyke Softball." The aesthetics of the game are further influenced by the team's philosophy of play and how each player views herself as an athlete in this world.

Switching gears somewhat, the next two chapters take on a few of the more difficult issues associated with dyke softball. Chapter 7 tackles the questions of why there is often a split in communities between jocks and feminists, where that split comes from, how women in these different parts of the community view one another, and why it's critical to close the gap when it's there. Chapter 8 looks at the interaction between dyke softball and some of the "isms": racism, sexism, heterosexism, and ageism. Not nearly so thorny but equally interesting is the relationship between lesbian softball teams and their sponsors—the subject of Chapter 9.

Finally, with a long history of importance to our community behind us, what lies in the future for dyke softball? Will it continue to play a valuable social function? Should it remain what it is, or should we work to change it, and how? The closing chapter of *Diamonds Are A Dyke's Best Friend* encourages us to envision softball in the lesbian community in the years ahead—a lesbian community that is rich and varied. I hope *Diamonds Are A*

Dyke's Best Friend is the first of many books to recognize and pay tribute to the role of softball in that rich and varied lesbian community.

Notes

1. Bill Figel, "Lesbians in World of Athletics," "Hustle Coach: Lesbianism Factor on Team," and "NU's Single Has a Cautious View," all in *Chicago Sun-Times*, June 16, 1986.

2. Joan C. Gondola and Toni Fitzpatrick, "Homophobia in Girls' Sports: Names That Can Hurt Us . . . ALL of Us," *Equal Play* (Spring/Summer 1985), p. 19.

Chapter 1

Full Count:
A Personal
Moment Of Truth

I don't remember ever actually learning to play softball. I recall learning how to catch, but I don't remember anyone ever telling me where to run if I hit the ball or where to throw when I fielded it. These things just seemed like something I always knew, like my own name. It has been difficult for me, therefore, to trace the halting progress of my softball game over the years and to witness how much my playing ability has deteriorated.

Starting with a second-place prize in the softball throw in fifth grade, my next softball memory is of me as a competent first baseman the summer before high school, catching the balls that Betty zinged in from her position at short, leaving my hand stinging. We played in a park-rec league on the scorching asphalt playgrounds of grade schools—not a good place to learn such advanced skills as sliding. But then, no one even attempted to teach us. Following that, after a ten- or fifteen-year hiatus from softball as I took a heavy academic courseload in high school and college, I became the best outfielder (left field—and sometimes center, simultaneously) of the worst team in a corporate league. I played there for two years, quitting only when I left the company. After a gap of another three or four years, I finally found a new team. But instead of being the best player on a bad team, I was one of the worst players on a good team—a team of seasoned high school and college ballplayers. The psychological adjustment has been difficult, each season marked by distinct ups and downs.

•After a season and a half of playing the bench, I finally got to play in right field with some regularity. (Not a bad position in our league, which boasts of any number of place hitters, as well as lefties.) Every game was filled with trepidation and excitement. Though my confidence was pretty low given that I hadn't been getting to play, I was nevertheless happy to be in there again. I was gratified that I got to play most of the games and, even more important, that I had made few if any errors out there in the field. But that gratification was diminished somewhat at the end of the season when I discovered a teammate had gone to the coach and said I made her (and apparently others) nervous out there in right field because I didn't approach the ball with confidence.

•One game, three or four of my friends from another team came to watch us play, and every time I was at bat, they yelled and screamed and cheered for me to a degree that was absurd and meant to provoke laughs from all concerned. While I knew it was in fun, it also made me nervous. It focused a lot of attention on me—and I am *not* a good batter.

•A friend of mine told me that I throw like a girl. I was crushed, of course, and disbelieving. "I have a good, strong throw," I thought. She told me she didn't mean it in a negative way, but to me it couldn't be anything but: "throwing like a girl" had always meant not throwing as well or as strongly as a boy. Finally, another friend helped me figure out that I didn't actually throw like a girl, rather that my throwing style was something of a hybrid between a girl's traditional approach and a boy's. I felt slightly better.

Accepting my malnourished athletic competence—and confidence—has been particularly difficult as an adult because I had always thought of myself as a naturally athletic person. Even my mother, when I was in high school, had suggested that I become a P.E. teacher. And so I have been none too anxious to let go of that image of myself. In addition, I have wanted very much to be accepted by my jock friends as a sister jock.

Diamonds Are A Dyke's Best Friend has enabled me to combine two of my greatest loves—writing and sports—in a way that both asserts my status (albeit shakily) as a jock and allows me to understand and better accept why I'm not the softball player I thought I was and would like to be. But working on the book has also reminded me that as long as I'm interested, as long as I'm willing to sweat, get dirty, and be part of a team, there will always be a place for me—and everyone like me—in dyke softball.

Chapter 2

From Out In Left Field: A Brief History

It is no secret that women have not exactly been a welcome addition to the world of athletics. One need only look at the exclusively male professional teams in baseball, football, and so on to see exactly how unwelcome women are. With the exception of the more "ladylike" individual sports of gymnastics, tennis, and swimming, women's ventures into professional sports have been greeted with derision, if they are noticed at all.

Sadly, this is not a recent phenomenon, a passing fad that we just have to wait out. The exclusion of women from sports is a long-entrenched tradition, going all the way back to ancient Greece where women were prevented from participating in the original Olympics. But the women, resourceful right from these early beginnings, organized the Herean Games in 776 B.C., a separate women's athletic competition.[1] The history of women and sports from that time to the present is filled with acts of discrimination by men—and acts of resistance by women. Some of that history, the history in this country from the 1800s on, is particularly valuable to examine because it set the stage for many of the discriminatory practices and unfounded allegations we still suffer under today.

Women And Sports In America: The 1800s To The 1980s

The 1800s

The history of women and sports is integrally linked with how society has historically viewed women, and men, in general. Consequently, any understanding of the evolution of the relationship between women and sports requires drawing on examples from various spheres.

One of the first areas in which women began opening up opportunities for themselves was in education, something very few women had access to—either formally or informally—before the nineteenth century. But by the 1840s, "[Catherine] Beecher, [Mary] Lyon, and [Emma] Willard had made it acceptable for women to teach and manage schools for women."[2] This is significant because it was through such schools that many women had their first experiences with sports.

While the value of exercise was becoming more and more accepted for boys by the mid- to late 1800s, girls were generally barred from such activities. There were two main reasons posited for their exclusion. The first had to do with medical concerns about the unsafeness of sports for the more delicate female; the second was that sports were deemed immodest for women.

In spite of such popular concerns, progressive, pioneering women educators saw value in providing some form of regular recreation for the young women in their charge. Harriet Isabel Ballintine of Vassar, for instance, wrote in

1898: "If refinement and quietness are but the results of weakness and inactivity, and a pronounced manner must necessarily be the outcome of a more vigorous life, we must be willing to sacrifice the former feminine attributes for the more precious possession of good health."[3]

Such sentiments as these were expressed in practice as well as verbally. At one school for young ladies in Connecticut, for example, "Miss Porter encouraged athletic activities beyond the scheduled daily walk and calisthenics. In the winter, the girls skated and sledded. Miss Porter bought a boat and had her manservant teach her and the students to row. In 1867 she yielded to student requests and permitted the girls to play baseball, *provided that the field was not visible from the road*" (italics mine).[4] Clearly not entirely free from the accepted constraints on female behavior, restrictions of all sorts were enforced: "[Students] learned that there were limits to what women should do and that social prescriptions decreed just how women should be active. For example, students dressed for tennis, [baseball], and country walks in school-approved ankle-length dresses. And although Miss Porter permitted tennis playing, since it promoted agility and strength, she forbade tennis tournaments. She did not approve of women's competition in tennis or in any field and refused to rank students by academic achievement. Women, she said, were to be known for their simplicity and humility, not for their accomplishments."[5]

Nevertheless, women's schools and colleges of the late 1800s defied the social conventions of the day, giving women a chance to play sports.

The creation of the bloomer at about this same time also contributed to introducing women to sports by providing them with greater freedom of movement than the contemporary restrictive clothing allowed. Though bloomers were greeted with great public disapproval because of their al-

leged indecency, they were soon made popular when the bicycle, which was rapidly and widely embraced by women, was introduced. In the face of the "cycling craze," "doctors and other custodians of female morality ultimately abandoned their crusade against the attire and activities of the 'lady cyclist.' Thus, cycling played an important part in liberating nineteenth-century women from rigid Victorian standards of acceptable dress and appropriate public behavior."[6]

The whole issue of physical exertion by women was extremely class-biased, however. While doctors and the whole of the upper and middle classes worried about the deleterious effects of physical activity on the health, daintiness, and moral demeanor of women from those classes, there was little concern over the long, hard hours worked by women on farms or for those—such as the daughters of farmers, immigrants, and freed slaves—who sweated and toiled in mills, factories, and as domestic servants in private homes. "For the affluent women, society prescribed lives of leisured indolence; for the working-class women, back-breaking toil."[7]

1900-1959

Where the fears of the nineteenth century centered on the emotional and physical fragility of women, those of the twentieth century were (and still are, to some extent) based more on the unfeminine nature of athletics: women might (perish the thought) develop muscles and competitive attitudes. Notwithstanding, the years immediately following World War I—perhaps owing to the fact that many women had been required to pursue traditionally masculine occupations in the name of the war effort—were surprisingly liberal in their attitudes toward women, encompassing not only sports but morality and fashion as well. (For examples of this, one need only look at the flappers of the 1920s.) The Depression years of the 1930s, however, saw a return to a greater conservatism, and sportswriters of the day never missed a chance to get in a jibe about the offensive and unfeminine qualities of female athletes. In 1936, for instance, sportswriter Paul Gallico said that "women looked beautiful in only eight of twenty-five sports. Some sports, including ball games, were out for making women perspire."[8] Nevertheless, in spite of societal disapproval, women were involved in organized physical activity more than ever before.

The next big leap forward for women and sports came in the 1940s when a war was once again responsible for opening, if only temporarily, doors that had previously been closed. Following the cycle of the previous war, however, the 1950s placed renewed emphasis on femininity and the supposed physical and intellectual inferiority of women. Still, women had gotten another toehold in the sports world.

1960-1988

This toehold was greatly strengthened in the 1960s by such things as the President's Council on Physical Fitness, which stressed the importance of fitness for both boys and girls—within limits for girls, of course. While the rising social consciousness of the sixties called into question a wide range of social biases and barriers, women were still not generally encouraged to strive for athletic excellence. Involvement in sports that was tolerated or even advocated for young girls (who were often half-affectionately known as *tomboys*) was actively discouraged once they became adolescents. Though expected to fulfill, albeit minimally, physical education requirements for school, adolescent girls were encouraged to put aside their tomboy ways and adopt more ladylike interests and a more feminine demeanor.

The next decade (the 1970s) brought with it the Women's Movement. But as Billie Jean King has noted, "I could never get the feminists of the early seventies to understand and integrate in their minds how sports fit."[9] While the Women's Movement did not take increased athletic opportunity as one of its major causes, its stress on equality for the sexes was nevertheless felt in sports as well. (Who can forget, for instance, the much publicized tennis match between Bobby Riggs and King, who it has been reported, "was a tomboyish softball enthusiast in her California youth, but. . . took to tennis because it seemed a more ladylike game.")[10] And by 1975, women had successfully argued for Title IX's support of equality in athletic education. Title IX, a stipulation of the Education Act of 1972, simply states: "No person in the United States shall, on the basis of sex, be excluded from participation in, be denied the benefits of, or be subjected to discrimination under any education program or activity receiving federal financial assistance." As a result of Title IX, women's sports received more funds; schools were required to make their physical education classes coed and provide a specific sport where a need was shown; and a proportional amount of scholarship funds was to be made available for women athletes based on the number of women in athletic programs. In general, most would agree that Title IX improved conditions for female athletes.

Then, in 1984, women's athletic programs suffered a setback when Title IX became essentially unenforceable. "In 1984, the Supreme Court decided in *Grove City College* v. *Ball* that only programs—not institutions—directly receiving federal funds would be under the jurisdiction of Title IX. There are very few, if any, athletic programs that directly receive federal funding. As a result, there is virtually no legal recourse under the federal Title IX statute for a woman who feels that athletic opportunities are being denied to her. Indeed, at the time of the Grove City decision, there were over sixty cases of Title IX violations under investigation. All were dropped." In addition, a number of universities and colleges cut specific women's sports or cut women's scholarships since the Grove City decision.[11] On March 22, 1988, however, "Title IX was restored to its original institution-wide power when the Senate and the House voted to override the President's veto and support the Civil Rights Restoration Act."[12] Only time will tell what the far-reaching effects of this legislation will be—and whether it will continue to be enforced.

Outside of the educational system, of course, there was never a Title IX to intercede, and athletic opportunities have consistently remained something less than equal. At municipal park facilities, for instance, women often find it difficult to gain access, preference being given to men's teams for basketball and volleyball courts and for softball fields. The park districts generally claim that access is given on the basis of demand or need; that is, they argue there just aren't that many women interested in using the facilities.[13] Another area where the inequalities are easily discerned is in the world of professional athletics, where women are most noticeable by their absence. Where you do find women in professional sports, they seldom receive either the pay or the publicity that their male counterparts do (with limited exceptions, again, for certain individual sports).

On the positive side, it is more acceptable than ever for women to be involved in sports. Physical fitness has actually become chic for women, though the sports that remain most "appropriate" (and the only ones in which they can make a living) are individual sports—particularly those that emphasize graceful motion and beauty and are designed to keep women lean and trim. With the exception of women involved in team sports or those who teach physical education, physically active women are much less likely to be viewed as freaks than they once were. There is still a tendency to consider women who are "too committed" to sports—who don't mind getting sweaty, dirty, and bruised in pursuit of athletic excellence—as unnatural. While there is clearly room for improvement, society is, in general, more supportive of women athletes than ever before in history.

To see how the current relationship between lesbians and softball came to be, it is necessary to examine more closely how and where softball fits into this overall history of women and sports in the United States.

Connecting Solidly: Women, Softball, And Baseball

Unlike baseball, the origins of which are often subject to debate, softball's origins are generally undisputed. Softball was born in November of 1887 at Chicago's Farragut Boat Club. The club members, bored while waiting for word of the results of the Yale-Harvard football game, took a boxing mitt and tied it tightly with twine into a ball shape. With this soft "ball," they began an impromptu game of indoor baseball.[14] Known variably as *mushball, indoor baseball, kittenball,* and *diamondball,* softball became so popular that within a few years there were organized clubs all over the city of Chicago. Softball was soon being played outdoors on playgrounds too small to allow for regulation-size baseball fields, and it rapidly spread throughout the Midwest and then the rest of the country.

During the early 1900s, when women were generally discouraged from any form of physical exertion, softball (along with women's basketball, or *lineball* as it was

called) was one of the few sports deemed suitable for
women because neither the large, soft ball nor the short
basepaths threatened physical harm or overexertion. Consequently, more women played softball than any other
team sport. Baseball, for example, was particularly frowned on for women, not only because of fears of injury but
also because of its seeming impropriety. These concerns
about appropriateness were probably based on the dubi-
ous charges of prostitution leveled at the teams of female
ballplayers that traveled across the United States and
Canada as early as 1879. Though the prostitution allegations are suspect, these barnstorming troops of lady ballplayers did violate a variety of accepted social customs.
A 1903 news item in the *Cincinnati Enquirer* reported,
for example: "A club of female ballplayers, claiming to be
from Brooklyn, N.Y., were jailed at Ft. Worth today for per-
sisting in playing a game with a club of young men, after
being notified by the police that the city park could not
be held for ballplaying purposes. The bloomer aggrega-
tion became 'brassy' and was run in . . . . In the corridors
and cells the girls raised a 'rough house.' They sang up-
to-date 'topical' songs, roasted the jail officials and male
prisoners, turned handsprings, stood on their heads,
walked on their hands, did high kicking, wide splits, and
other startling performances."[15]

Other aspects of softball's growth were also significant
in shaping it as a sport played particularly by women. For
one thing, "the development of women's softball differed
from the development of other women's team sports in
that it was less strictly controlled by educational poli-
cies."[16] Played primarily in summer and in public parks,
softball was not governed by school administrators. This
looser control meant that softball, unlike any other team
sport played by women, evolved without imposing different rules or playing methods on men and women. In ad-

dition, as in no other team activity, women had an opportunity to play toward a national championship.

Factors that contributed to the growth of softball in general also had an effect on its popularity with women. Among these factors was the birth of industrial recreation which was a part of the social reform movement at the turn of the century. As inhumane working conditions were exposed, employers were pressured to subsidize a variety of facilities and programs to help alleviate those conditions. Industrially sponsored recreation was one such program, and often included softball. And during the Depression some thirty years later, when greater numbers of women were working, women's industrial softball teams were not at all uncommon. Another factor that contributed to the rise of the softball, particularly during the Depression, was that it was inexpensive to play. Social reform programs and the minimal expense involved in playing softball were probably in large part responsible for transforming it from a sport for the upper classes, in its Farragut Boat Club days, to a sport associated primarily with the working class.

Women's Professional Baseball

But perhaps the most interesting outgrowth of softball's popularity with women was a women's professional *baseball* league from 1943-54. Though women today do not generally play baseball (except, perhaps, as children), and the league was all but erased from history, the women of the All-American Girls Professional Baseball League (AAGPBL) were pioneers in the world of women's sports: they broke ground for building a positive image of athletic women, particularly women playing team sports. They were the foremothers, the role models many of us never knew we had. Where did these women come from? How did this league—the longest lived of any women's professional athletic league—begin?

Many of the women who would eventually play ball in the AAGPBL were playing softball in park district or industrial leagues when Philip K. Wrigley, owner of the Chicago Cubs and the Wrigley Chewing Gum Company first conceived of a "girls'" ball league. Fearing that the projected manpower crisis during World War II would adversely affect men's professional baseball, Wrigley created the AAGPBL as a substitute entertainment. It had become a patriotic duty for women to tackle a variety of previously male-dominated occupations in the 1940s. Most went to work in factories or offices. Some entered the sports arena—as jockeys, football coaches, umpires, caddies, and ballplayers.

The AAGPBL was set up as a nonprofit organization governed by a board of trustees: Wrigley, Paul Harper (an attorney for the Cubs), and Branch Rickey (general manager of the Brooklyn Dodgers). Arthur Meyerhoff, a principal advertising agent for the Wrigley Company, was also enlisted to help with the League. The stated purpose of this organization was to build morale, raise money for war bonds, develop youth programs, and visit service hospitals.

Originally, Wrigley intended the League to play in National League ballparks on off-dates, but national defense blackout regulations and other complications prevented him from carrying this out. (The AAGPBL did, however, manage to play at some of these ballparks for exhibition games.) Instead, four Midwestern towns, which were war production centers where men's and women's softball had been popular in the 1930s, were selected as AAGPBL team sites: Racine and Kenosha, Wisconsin; Rockford, Illinois; and South Bend, Indiana. At its height, the League had as many as ten teams, all in the Midwest.

The players, however, came from across the country and Canada. Thirty scouts had searched baseball and softball diamonds for outstanding athletes. Tryout camps were set up, to which hundreds of women flocked. Seventy-five women were picked from these regional tryouts to attend final tryouts at Wrigley Field. Sixty of them were selected to staff the original four teams.

Initially, the League was known as the All-American Girls' Softball League, though the game was actually a hybrid of softball and baseball, with its softball-sized ball and expanded diamond size and baseball rules. From there the game evolved rapidly, the ball becoming smaller and harder, the diamond larger, the pitching faster and, by 1948, overhand, until it was not much different from regulation baseball. By 1945, the League had officially changed its name to the All-American Girls' Baseball League. The *Professional* was added some time later.

Attendance figures, especially from 1943-49, attest to the popularity of this brand of major league ball. In 1948, for instance, the Racine Belles and Rockford Peaches both outdrew the populations of their cities. As former AAGPBL player Pepper Paire said, "People may have come out the first time just for laughs and to see the legs, but they kept coming back—and that was because we played good baseball."[17]

To substantiate this assertion, one need only look at the statistics kept on these women (Sophie Kurys's 201 stolen bases—out of 203 attempts—in a single season, to cite one particularly impressive example) and newspaper clippings of the day, which reported such items as offers of minor league contracts on men's teams for Dottie Kamenshek (described, by Wally Pipp, former New York Yankee, as the best fielding first baseman he'd ever seen) and for Eleanor Engle. Kamenshek reportedly refused the offer, and Engle's was hastily withdrawn when a rule was quickly devised barring the signing of women as players. There were also praises from players from the men's major leagues, such as former Chicago Cub Charlie Grimm, who once said of another player, "Dottie Schroeder would be worth $50,000 if she were a man."[18]

For women such as Paire, who would "rather play ball than eat," the AAGPBL was a dream come true. And for some, it was even more than that: it was a way off the farm, out of the small town, out of poverty. Reasons like these made the women willing to put up with the stringent regulations imposed on them by the League: no short haircuts; no shorts, slacks, drinking, or smoking in public; dating only with a chaperon's permission; and strict bedtime rules. The uniforms were somewhat impractical dresses with flared skirts, and players were required to attend charm school—conducted by Helena Rubinstein—for lessons on hairstyling, makeup, and deportment.

Shirley Jameson, outfielder for the Kenosha Comets (1943-46), has said of charm school: "As far as charm school went, it was fine for what it was, but the [charm school] women didn't seem to be tuned into what we had to do. . . . Some of it was apropos, but a lot of it you just couldn't use playing baseball. We had one chaperon who really went overboard, and when someone was running up to bat, she would say, 'You don't have any lipstick on!' Well, you know, that's the last thing in the world someone in a ball game is thinking about. She said it to me once when I was coming up to the plate in a game-winning situation! I don't know whether I had lipstick on or not, but at that point, I could have cared less, I was playing the game."[19]

Though such restrictions and requirements seem ridiculous and sexist today, the players looked at it very pragmatically at the time: it was what they had to do to play ball, so they did it. Today, most are firmly convinced that the success of the League owed much to this stress on "femininity"—a view clearly shared by the League's administration. Bearing in mind the variety of accusations leveled at the Bloomer Girls, Wrigley sought to maintain an image of propriety for his league. He was also concerned that no one mistake his players for men in dresses and that no one accuse them of lesbianism.[20]

Unfortunately, in the long run, looking feminine and playing great ball weren't enough. The end of the war brought with it a return to more traditionally sex-defined roles, and, by the 1950s, a woman's place was once again in the home. Other factors contributing to the demise of the AAGPBL included drastic cuts in the promotional budget, reduced game attendance because of changing recreational habits (more TV, travel), the reduction of the talent pool because of the switch from softball to baseball, administrative and League structure changes, and the loss of key players because of injuries, retirement, and recruitment by semipro women's softball leagues. In 1954, the women of the AAGPBL turned in their uniforms and went home.

That was nearly the last anyone heard about the AAGPBL until 1982 when the League held its first reunion. Feminist historians rediscovered the AAGPBL and began recording its history in articles for both professional and popular magazines, as well as in pamphlets, baseball cards, and video documentaries. Unfortunately, the All-American Girls Professional Baseball League has yet to receive the recognition it deserves from the Baseball Hall of Fame in Cooperstown, New York. Though it has finally gotten permanent space in an eight-by-eight-foot exhibit commemorating women in baseball (that is, any woman with any connection to baseball, including owners, managers, and umpires), the AAGPBL hasn't been recognized as another official major league. But no one involved, neither former players nor fans, has given up yet!

Women's Professional Softball

In 1975, Billie Jean King—along with three male executives and star softball pitcher Joan Joyce—founded the International Women's Professional Softball League (IWPSL). But while the IWPSL and AAGPBL had a few things in common—a handful of teams at the start (six for the IWPSL, four for the AAGPBL), a talent pool of amateur and semipro softball players, and uniforms that left legs bare —there were probably more differences than similarities.

The obvious difference, of course, was *softball* versus *baseball*. In addition, however, where the AAGPBL lasted over ten years, the IWPSL barely lasted four. Where AAGPBL players were paid salaries that were competitive with those of their day (to lure them from high-paying factory jobs), IWPSL players got about $1,000-$3,000 per season (roughly $7-$21 per game), for which they were contractually bound to attend "Meet the Fans" ceremonies, perform at promotional exhibitions, run softball clinics, and play an average of 140 games per year. Where the AAGPBL received tremendous media coverage and spectator support (especially in its early years), the IWPSL got little of either. Where the AAGPBL had one central, seasoned owner, the IWPSL had separate, sometimes inadequate, franchises. This resulted in inequalities from team to team not only in the amount of publicity each team received, but also in player salaries and management effectiveness. Of all the differences between the two leagues, the most interesting one to examine is why the AAGPBL succeeded while the IWPSL failed. There is no single simple answer.

One might be tempted to guess that the women of the IWPSL weren't as skilled ball players as their AAGPBL counterparts had been. That would be incorrect. While the two leagues assuredly played different types of ball, their skill levels were comparable. In one of the few instances of media coverage that the softball league got, for instance, Michael Kazin of the *Berkeley Barb* said of them: "They field almost flawlessly and pitch with both speed and control."[21] Why, then, the lack of spectator and media interest?

On the one hand, while women athletes were much more common and/or accepted in the seventies than they were in the forties, on the other hand, it was the very novelty of those World War II and postwar female ballplayers that whipped up interest in them. Furthermore, the powerful and wealthy backing of the Wrigley empire ensured better publicity for the AAGPBL than was available for the IWPSL. It has also been postulated that softball is more a participant sport than a spectator sport.[22] Moreover, the conditions that prevailed during—and no doubt prompted—the declining years of the women's baseball league (i.e., expanded recreational options) continued and had probably increased by the seventies when the IWPSL folded.

I would also suggest that athletic women of the forties, while perhaps viewed as oddities, were not looked on with as much suspicion and contempt as their counterparts in the seventies. This speculation is based on two things. First, with the emergence of the contemporary Women's Movement, there was a backlash against strides made by women toward greater independence, especially in what was considered the sacred domain of sports. Second, while lesbianism was neither unheard of nor socially accepted in the forties, if one maintained a low profile—that is, looked and acted feminine—it was easier to pass then than it was in the post-Stonewall years, when any woman functioning outside of traditionally female roles was much more likely to be suspect. (It must be remembered that while the women of the AAGPBL, like the women of the IWPSL, were performing in the traditionally male arena of professional sports, it was not an uncommon role during a time of manpower shortages created by the war.) Both of these factors may have contributed to more of a distaste for the ballplayers of the seventies.

Whether the players of either league were actually lesbians has little bearing on the ultimate success or failure of these two leagues—it is the public's perception of them that counts. And both leagues were clearly aware of this and concerned about the image they conveyed. The AAGPBL, as discussed earlier, dealt with the image problem by sending their women to charm school. The IWPSL also guarded its image carefully. For instance, although many of its players were, in fact, lesbians,[23] three women at a softball training camp sponsored by Joan Joyce and her Connecticut Falcons were asked to leave for allegedly demonstrating overt lesbian behavior. While it wasn't made clear what constituted this behavior, speculation focused on having unshaven legs, reading a copy of *Lesbian Images* (Jane Rule) in public, and one woman massaging another's temples. For the AAGPBL, creating an image of femininity worked. For the IWPSL, even outright disavowal of lesbianism wasn't enough: public perceptions had changed.

Women On The Ball: Some Recent Facts

•Softball remains the number one team sport played by women. Out of the twenty-seven million softball players in this country, about five million of them are women.[24]

•Joan Joyce holds the record for the fastest pitch in softball at 118 mph (set in 1966), compared to Jack Newman's 108 mph (in 1962), the record pitch for men. This puts the women's record in this area at 109.3% of the men's record.[25]

•A woman, Pam Postema, finally made it to Class AAA baseball in 1983—as an umpire.

•A women's baseball team, the Sun Sox, applied for admission to the Class A Florida State League in 1984. They were unable to dismantle pro baseball's sex barrier.[26]

Dusting Off The Plate:
How We Found Our Way Home

Looking back at the history of women and sports—especially softball—and at the history of society's relationship with lesbians, the questions "Why not lesbians and some *other* sport?" and "*Why* is softball so important?" become linked. They are so intricately linked, in fact, that it is difficult to know where to begin answering. But let's try coming at it this way.

"By the 1930s, sex and marriage manuals popularized Freudian psychology and brought an end to the 'age of innocence' regarding close relationships between women."[27] From that time forward, life in these United States has been particularly difficult for lesbians. So. In the thirties and forties, when social outlets for women in general were extremely limited—in the days before women's organizations burgeoned and when "nice" women didn't go out alone, especially at night and *especially* to bars—softball, as one of the only sports available to women, also became a major social avenue.

There are probably several reasons, in addition to the more general ones just indicated, why softball was a magnet for lesbians. One is that as single women, lesbians were no doubt in the work force in higher percentages than their heterosexual counterparts. In those days, especially if they were married, straight women generally didn't work outside the home except in cases of dire emergency or unless they were from poor families. Therefore, during the height of the industrial softball league, which drew its players from the work force, it stands to reason that a good percentage of those on the teams were lesbians. Another reason softball was probably populated by lesbians is that to be a female athlete one needs certain special qualities. These qualities include both mental and physical strength, the ability to go against social norms, and a certain independence of spirit—qualities that the lesbian out on her own, supporting herself, would be likely to have to one degree or another.

As lesbians were drawn in greater numbers to softball teams because of their greater presence in the work force, because of social conditions, and because of their more independent natures, it became an unofficial place to meet other lesbians. It was not something people talked about—they just knew. As Barbara Grier of Naiad Press has said, "In the early years, softball was. . . the only organized, programmed, regimented, routinized activity that the lesbian community at large engaged in—by tacit understanding." And in the fifties and early sixties, when in addition to the stigma attached to single women going to bars there were the raids on lesbian bars to contend with, the softball game was one of the best, safest, and most socially acceptable places to meet and socialize.

Even for the women who were not ball players, softball was an important social event. Again, Barbara Grier: "It was a place to go where you knew there would be dykes," she said, pointing out that there is a lesbian *audience* for softball games as well as lesbian *players*. One woman I spoke with recalled traveling at that time with her lover; neither of them were ball players. In a strange city, looking for something to do with themselves one evening, the woman suggested they head out to the ball parks. "What on earth for?" her lover asked. "Because that's where the lesbians will be," she answered.

In many rural areas today it is still the case that softball is one of the only places, by "tacit understanding," to meet other dykes. And even in urban centers, dyke softball is a tradition that is a viable alternative to the bars and an outlet for women who are not inclined toward lesbian cultural and political activism.

Notes

1. Patricia J. Murphy, "Sport and Gender," in Wilbert Marcellus Leonard II, *A Sociological Perspective of Sport*, 2d ed. (Minneapolis, Minn.: Burgess Publishing, 1984), p. 193.

2. Louise L. Stevenson, "Sarah Porter Educates Useful Ladies, 1847-1900," *Winterthur Portfolio* 18, no. 1 (Spring 1983): 40; also, see Stephanie L. Twin, "Jock and Jill: Aspects of Women's Sports History in America, 1870-1940" (Ph.D. thesis, Rutgers University, 1978), chap. 1.

3. Allen Guttmann, "Women's Sports," in his *A Whole New Ball Game: An Interpretation of American Sports* (Chapel Hill: University of North Carolina Press, 1988), p. 144.

4. Stevenson, p. 44; also, see Murphy (p. 195), who points out that in the late 1800s, "Men's sports were in the public sphere, but most women's collegiate sports took place within the walls of women's colleges (often closed to the male public to avoid 'indecent exposures')."

5. Stevenson, p. 48.

6. Helen Lenskyj, *Out of Bounds: Women, Sport and Sexuality* (Toronto: Women's Press, 1986), p. 19.

7. Barbara Ehrenreich and Deirdre English, *Complaints and Disorders: The Sexual Politics of Sickness* (Old Westbury, N.Y.: Feminist Press, 1973), p. 11.

8. Stephanie L. Twin, ed., *Out of the Bleachers: Writings on Women and Sport* (Old Westbury, N.Y.: Feminist Press, 1979), p. xxxiv.

9. Quoted in Michele Kort, "*Ms.* Conversation," *Ms.* (February 1988), p. 60.

10. William J. Baker, *Sports in the Western World* (Totowa, N.J.: Rowman & Littlefield, 1982), p. 296.

11. Candace Lyle Hogan, "What's the Future for Women's Sports?" *Women's Sports and Fitness* 9, no. 6 (June 1987): 44.

12. "Power of Title IX Restored," *Headway: The Women's Sports Foundation Newsletter* (Spring 1988).

13. See, e.g., Lynda Gorov, "Parks Shutting Us Out, Women Softballers Say," *Chicago Sun-Times*, April 9, 1987; and Linda Johanek, "Sports Seen: Softball Scores with Area Women," *Today's Chicago Woman*, August 1986.

14. Felicia E. Halpert, "How the Game Was Invented," *Women's Sports and Fitness* 9, no. 7 (July 1987): 34. One dissenting view on this widely accepted version of the birth of softball seems to be Harvey Frommer (*Sports Roots* [New York: Atheneum, 1979], p. 151): "It is alleged that firehouse spare-time inspired Lewis [Robert, Minneapolis firefighter] to innovate what was at first an indoor game." Frommer also gives softball's date of origin as 1895. Interestingly, this is the date that Halpert gives as the "time a version of the outdoor game was being played in Minneapolis, where it was popular among the city's fire fighters" (p. 34). Another thing that Frommer says in his encyclopedia of sports origins is that Robert is credited with making the first softball. Given that Frommer's "date of origin" is eight years later than the generally accepted date, perhaps he has confused Robert's making (manufacturing?) of the first softball with inventing the game. Note that this needs further investigation.

15. "Bloomer Ball Tossers: Were Pinched and Raised a Rough House in Texas Jail," *Cincinnati Enquirer*, July 20, 1903.

16. Merrie A. Fidler, "The Establishment of Softball as a Sport for American Women, 1900-1940," in *Her Story in Sport*, ed. Reet Howell (West Point, N.Y.: Leisure Press, 1982), p. 528.

17. Jay Feldman, "Perspective," *Sports Illustrated* (June 10, 1985).

18. Sharon L. Roepke, *Diamond Gals* (Marcellus, Mich.: A.A.G.B.L. Cards, 1986), p. 10.

19. Feldman.

20. Roepke, p. 11.

21. Michael Kazin, "Hottest Baseball in the Bay," *Berkeley Barb* (June 21-July 4, 1979).

22. Interview with Ron Hagen, director of marketing, Major League Volleyball, January 1987.

23. "A professional player, Diane Kallium [San Jose Sunbirds/Rainbow], when asked how many of the women in pro-softball are lesbians, replied, 'Virtually all' " (Janisis and Laurie Bach, "Diamonds Are A Dyke's Best Friend," *Lesbian Tide* 6, no. 6 [May/June 1977]: 22). Although no "official" thanks are due (since I named the book before coming across the article), I appreciate my sister softball players who were thinking about lesbians and the game before I was.

24. *Sports Illustrated Sports Poll '86*, conducted by Lieberman Research Inc. (New York: Time, Inc., 1986), pp. 43-44; Ed Zolna and Mike Conklin, *Mastering Softball* (Chicago: Contemporary Books, Inc., 1981); Ellen W. Gerber et al., *The American Woman in Sport* (Reading, Mass.: Addison-Wesley, 1974), p. 117.

25. Jonathan Ullyot, comp., "Where the Women Are," *Women's Sports and Fitness* 9, no. 6 (June 1987): 56.

26. "A Diamond These Girls' Best Friend," *Daily Star*, September 18, 1984.

27. Lenskyj, p. 73.

Chapter 3

On Deck: The Softball Experience Before We "Knew"

I remember being out there every day after school [playing ball] till it was dark and having my mother actually drag me into the house, saying, "Get inside." Because all I wanted to do was play ball all the time. (Olivia)

If society is still not supportive of girls and women getting involved in team sports, how and why did so many of us learn to play softball so well? Where did our love for the game come from? As different as we are, our early experiences are surprisingly similar—especially concerning those who encouraged us. And those who didn't.

Our First Cheering Sections
Parents

As with most things in early childhood, our parents often played a major role in how we related to softball. What surprised me is that their role tended to be positive. Many of us, though certainly not all, had parents who encouraged our early athletic endeavors, parents who did more than simply allow us to play—they often taught the game to us, played with us, bought our equipment, and generally applauded our efforts. Such parental involvement is apparently common among female athletes, as parents are capable of screening us, to some extent, from the social sanctions against physical activity for young girls and women. Studies have shown, in fact, that family attitudes are one of the most significant factors accounting for female athletic participation.[1]

Dads

Missy Myers: "I remember some of the best moments in the brief, shining period of my life when my dad actually paid some attention to me were in softball, when I was ten and, swallowing my disdain for *soft*ball (having played baseball with the boys up to that point), finally joined a team. I was a pitcher, and out of the clear blue my dad began playing catch with me, working on my delivery and control. He was an engineer and took great delight in keeping elaborate statistics on the players on my team, meticulously comparing my accuracy to Paula's speed to Mary's fielding in various situations. It was great. He also took me hunting and fishing with him a couple of times that year, and all in all, I couldn't believe my luck. Alas, my enthusiasm frightened him—I learned, years later, that he feared he was influencing/encouraging me in a 'masculine' direction (my coming out later in life confirmed his fears)—and he quickly faded back into his workaholism."

Ellen: "[I] Played a lot of 'catch' with my father."

J. T.: "We always had spare wood around the farm (flatwood) that we'd taken down from buildings or something like that. So I'd stand in the driveway and bat

SUMMER'S END

Father: How'd everything go at the ballgame?

Uncle Dudley: Great! Kathy got to pitch 'cuz old Eddie hurt his knee.

Father: Kathy got to pitch?

Uncle Dudley: Yeah! As a matter of fact, she threw the winning pitch.

Father: Is that a fact!

Uncle Dudley: Yeah! Ray Don tried to slap one by and she jumped on it like a little frog.

Father: Nothing happened to upset her?

Uncle Dudley: No—last time I saw her she was grinnin' like a mule eatin' briars.

Mother [to father]: As long as you keep encouraging her to play baseball and to build clubhouses and model airplanes, she's not going to know what it is to be a girl. Don't you see that it's just confusing her?

Kathy: Daddy, I got to pitch in the last game.

Father: Yeah, I heard that. Dudley said you won the game.

Kathy: I did. I threw the ball into home and the runner was tagged comin' in from third.

Father: Now you know that your mother's real upset you didn't show up for your beauty parlor appointment. What happened? Why'd you do that?

Kathy: I hate curls! They're sissy.

Father: Oh you couldn't be sissy—I don't care what they did to your hair. Sissy's a coward. You're as brave as anybody I know.

Kathy: I don't like bein' a girl. Girls don't have any fun.

Father: Well, you know, it's not always easy being a boy either. We all got to do things we don't want to do sometimes. What's really important, sweetie, is what's deep, deep, deep down inside you, way down inside of you—nobody can ever take that away from you ever—I don't care what they do to you—I don't care if they shave your head. You know, if the world was perfect, nobody would care what you did as long as you didn't hurt anybody. The world's not perfect. It ain't perfect.

(Selected scenes from a 1987 half-hour movie about a young girl, Kathy, in Arkansas in the early 1950s, written, produced, and directed by Beth Brickell.)

gravel—swing away at the gravel. Dad would say to me, 'If you hit the barn roof, I'll give you a quarter.' Or, "If you hit the shed, I'll give you a milkshake.' So I used to swat away at the stones in the driveway, swing away with the board, see how far I could hit it. . . . [And then], when I first got involved with softball. . .I remember Dad taking me in the backyard and putting up badminton poles to define the batter's swinging area. Then he'd be the catcher, and we'd practice pitching. He'd call strikes or balls or how close they were to the side of the plate."

Cathy: "My father was my best coach."

Fathers were far and away the most supportive parent of our early softball experiences. Over and over, women indicated to me that their fathers had taught them how to play and worked with them on their skills. Research also confirms the positive role of fathers in their daughters' softball playing.[2] For women whose fathers weren't in the picture, other adult male role models often took their place in sports endeavors. Louise Hernandez, for instance, learned the game from an uncle who had noted her interest in the game. In my own case, though father figures were a little scarce, I do have distinct memories of playing catch with a male friend of my mother's. It was, in fact, on one such occasion, when I was six or seven and missed the ball, getting hit squarely in the nose, that I wondered why they called it *soft* ball!

Moms

Kathy Phillips: "I wanted a baseball bat for my 12th or 13th birthday. Adults said that this was not an appropriate gift for a young lady, but my mother bought it for me anyway. She never discouraged my 'nonlady-like' behaviors."

No doubt, there are and have always been mothers who have gone out and played softball or catch with their daughters, but none of the women that I know or spoke with have ever mentioned such mothers.[3] Still, those of us who didn't have mothers who actively discouraged our ballplaying, or who were completely indifferent, at least had mothers who were supportive in less participatory ways. Some, like Kathy Phillips's mother, bought us the necessary equipment. Others, like my mom, showed a lot of interest in our softball achievements without actually becoming involved.

I often wonder, especially as more lesbians choose to be mothers, what the experiences, the memories, will be like for the next generation of young women. Lesbian feminist poet Pat Parker, for instance, insists that her daughters will not only be encouraged to do well in school but also to participate in some sport—any sport. At this writing, her daughters seem pretty interested in softball. Will they someday recall fondly, "My mother was my best coach"?

Brothers And Others

Laurie: "I used to play a lot with my brother and his friends while in grammar school. It was always very competitive because he was a few years younger than I, so we were pretty equal in ability. (I'm glad they let me play with them—otherwise I wouldn't be at the level of proficiency I am at now.)"

Connie: "We used to play softball on a vacant lot outside my home. I would play with mainly male (some younger) friends. My greatest thrill was that I could play better than them considering they were *males*."

V.: "The girls wouldn't play with me, so I had to play with the boys as a kid. All the boys in the neighborhood used to play softball, so I started playing with them."

Mary Boutilier and Lucinda SanGiovanni: "We were vaguely aware of the fact that games and sports were for boys. Most of the time we were the only girls playing. We dismissed this with the rationalization that the rest of the girls just were not interested or talented enough."[4]

Ellen Heimbuck: "It seems ironic that I learned the game from so many men; I'm definitely grateful though. One of my earliest memories is of me pitching when I was in second grade. I was playing with and against much older boys. (No girls.) One of the boys hit a hard come-back, and it hit me in the head. Well, it bounced just right so I followed the play and got the boy out. They were all shocked that I continued to play."

Among the men we learned the game from, many of us can also count both brothers and neighborhood boys. In fact, this may very well be the most common thing that softball dykes (or any athletic women) share. A 1985 study by Miller Lite of over 1,500 athletic women found that women who are now or have been most active in organized sports played mostly with boys or mixed gender groups (as opposed to mostly with other girls) when they were children.[5] Over and over again, when recalling how they learned to play softball (or in many cases, baseball), most lesbians mention having played with boys.

Missy Myers: "None of my female relatives or friends were particularly athletic, so I spent most of my childhood running with the boys in the neighborhood. Consequently, I started out playing baseball, not softball, and with boys several years older than myself. Eleven-year-old boys are not distinguished by their great tolerance or warmth, particularly not for girls, and especially not for little girls, but to their credit, they let me play. Sort of. My earliest athletic memory is of playing hotbox with the boys next door (I was six or seven, they were eleven), racing back and forth between the bases while they threw the baseball as hard as they could at the back of my head. 'Oops,' they would say, and laugh, and I knew they were trying to get me to quit. So I didn't."

G is for Gretchen, who knew at age seven.

Of course, we weren't always welcomed with open arms by the boys. Often the reception we got was just the opposite, as Missy's experience illustrates. It seems that boys get indoctrinated into the male world of sports at a very early age and then do their best to keep it a closed club. But in spite of their efforts to dissuade, many of us remained persistent.

Part of this perseverance for some of us had to do with a lack of other options. As Jackie from Minneapolis said, "When I was a kid in grade school, that's all we did [played softball]. Our playground equipment was a ball and a bat. If you wanted to have any fun at all, that's what you did."[6] But for many, though we probably could not have articulated it at the time, we played because somehow we believed it was our destiny: we were good at sports—sports were what we were meant to do. J. T., for instance, frequently says, "I felt that I was born to be a ballplayer," and was bitter for years about that stolen opportunity. But as kids, most of us didn't fully realize that the road to professional athletics would never be open to us in our lifetimes. So we worked hard toward that goal, fighting the odds.

The Hostile Crowd
Childhood

Susan Begg: "[My] earliest significant memory [is of] being turned down to try out for Little League when [I was] seven years old—I was crushed to be told only boys could play."

Louise Hernandez: "There was one incident—I must have been ten years old. It started raining and drizzling. My mom wasn't real supportive with my playing softball. I mean, I had to ride my bike to practice, ride my bike to my ball games. And my mom came to [one] game—the middle of the game—and made my brother get out and call me off the field because they didn't call the game [and] it was drizzling out. My brother was pissed that he had to come get me out of the game—he was only eleven. She called me out of the game; they had to stop it [while I left the field]. I was one of the better players on the team, and I had to be pulled from the game because of my mom. It was humiliating. . . . My mom wasn't sports-minded. That's all there was to it. She let me do it because I was a kid and she felt sorry for me because [she and my father had] divorced."

Meryl Moskowitz: "My earliest memory dates back to kindergarten (1956) when I realized I wasn't allowed to join the boys during a baseball game at recess and, instead, was relegated to the swings."

Rhoda Rover: "It was a crushing blow to me, the best baseball player in the neighborhood, to find I couldn't try out for the Little League. I have never played a sport seriously again until [1976]."[7]

From "Lesbian Athletes" article: "When I was eleven . . . I played baseball with the kids until mom would yell at me to come eat. And I used to kick their butts, man! They couldn't hit a fly I couldn't catch; I could hit flies they couldn't catch. Then, when it came time for Little League, who was in the stands watching those little turkeys? And it pisses me off now that it didn't piss me off then. But I had no reason to be pissed off, because I did not know I was being cheated, that something was wrong. I always wanted to be a boy because I couldn't do those neat things boys could. Now I'm glad I'm not a boy, because only girls can be lesbians."[8]

Although each of these stories is slightly different, one point is clear: there is no easy road to athletics for girls and women. For some women, one or both parents obstruct their path. For others, while their families are supportive, the system—Little League—keeps them out.[9] Some women persevered and played whatever sports they could, when and wherever they could. Others gave in under the mounting pressure to be ladylike—especially as they approached or entered adolescence.

Adolescence

Bea: "[I] learned how to pitch and catch hardball with my father and brother 5th-7th grades, at home only [because I] found out—was told by [my] peers—in 5th grade, girls didn't play softball at recess, they watched. So I watched, and in high school and college I played tennis for my schools. When I became a feminist (during law school), I played softball again for the first time since forever and now I like how much I like playing."

Maryhel Hibben: "My parents never attended any game I participated in . . . . They refused to give me any support for my achievements in sports, probably because it is too tomboyish and unladylike for their beliefs."[10]

Pat Parker: "Within Black culture, there was a real strong emphasis put to me that once I hit puberty [I was supposed to] move away from mannish or boyish things. Like, 'Well, you're not supposed to play ball with the boys anymore.' "

J. T.: "My parents were extremely supportive of my being involved in athletics. . . . When I got interested in softball during the high school years, Mom and Dad would always come to my Thursday night league. And when that Thursday night team turned into a traveling team (the Oxford Merchants), they would come to all the games on weekends. When the Oxford Merchants folded, the only other team that I'd think of playing on was the Springfield Robinettes. They were our [the Oxford Merchants] true competitors. They were up in Springfield, Ohio, which was an hour-and-a-half drive up and an hour-and-a-half drive back. When the Springfield Robinettes asked me if I'd play, my folks [gave their permission] and let me go up twice a week for practices. And the Springfield Robinettes played tournaments every single weekend, and I traveled with the team."

Mary Boutilier and Lucinda SanGiovanni: "It was as adolescents that we, like countless other tomboys, were taught that the sweaty, vigorous world of sports had to be abandoned in order for us to lay claim to a feminine identity."[11]

Those of us who were able to live a carefree childhood as tomboys found, as our teen years closed in, that different behaviors were now expected of us. The tree climbing, ballplaying, and daredevil acts that everyone thought were cute when we were in grade school were definitely frowned on as childish and, more significantly, unladylike the minute we entered the doors of the junior high or high school.

That was certainly true in my case. I don't recall a specific incident related to softball, but the messages came in other ways. In ninth grade, for example, I remember asking for a bicycle—nothing fancy, just something without balloon tires and beat-up fenders! My parents insisted that I would lose interest in it as soon as I entered high school, where I presumably would discover boys, dances, and femininity in all its guises. (So there's no lost sleep over this heart-rending tale, I finally did get the bike—a girl's Schwinn with coaster brakes—but not without a lot of arguments.)

Some girls—like J. T. and another friend of mine, She-Her, for whom softball was actually a way to be popular in high school—escaped such parental and social pressures to be feminine and played softball all through school. But they were exceptions to the rule. A study of female high school athletes confirms this, finding that mothers and peers of both sexes judged softball to be one of the least desirable sports for female competitors.[12]

"Then there are the subtle discouragements: the unenlightened suspicion that a woman's interest in athletics violates the docile female stereotypes and indicates lesbianism (remember the rumors about gym teachers?)."[13] Certainly, there were very few of us who were oblivious to the stigma attached to avid athletic participation and who didn't at least consider the consequences before we decided to remain active in sports. Thomas Tutko, a psychologist at San Jose State University, summed up the progression of labels attached to athletic women this way: "A male athlete is glorified . . . but think what happens to a girl. First she's called a tomboy, then a freako, then a lesbian."[14] Most of us—especially those of us who are old enough to remember what it was like before the Women's Movement and the health craze made sports "O.K." for women—succumbed to this pressure and stopped much or all of our athletic involvement in high school and college or, if we didn't, went out of our way to look and act feminine off the field.

What is truly amazing about all of this, though, is that so many of us who were prevented from playing softball, whether as children or adolescents, finally found our way back. Obviously it is a game we fell in love with, for many reasons. But not every dyke's heart was won by softball.

The Budding Nonjock

Liz: "My mother required me to play softball hoping it would improve my coordination. She let me quit after the nun who was coaching got hit with a bat and broke her jaw. Nineteen girls [went out for that team], and I was on the third string. I *was* the third string."

Mariah Burton Nelson: " 'I hate competition!' some friends have said to me. These are the women who were never taught how to throw or catch a ball, and I don't blame them. As an untrained musician, I know that if my childhood had been filled with music competitions, and I were chosen last for music teams and humiliated in front of other great musicians, I would resent both music and competition. Who enjoys doing things poorly?"[15]

Rhonda Craven: "When I was a kid, about five or six years old, my father wanted me to be a jock on a certain level. But I was getting mixed messages because what would happen is, he would teach me how to do things like play softball, box, things like that. But then if I got hurt, I wasn't supposed to cry about it because that was just part of playing these games. And I didn't agree with that. But particularly with softball, it was very painful in some respects. What he would want to do is go out to the park, and we'd have a softball, and he would fire it at me. I've always had little hands (still do), and I wouldn't have a glove, and it would hurt. So I got to the point where I would just avoid the ball. It still carries over to now. . . . I haven't developed any skills as far as catching and throwing balls because it was not something I was interested in—it was always associated with hurting. Although he would badger me about it and badger me, I would just retreat that much more. So as time went on, he finally realized this was a waste of time and he'd leave me alone about it. From that, I've just never had an interest."

At first glance, the catalyst for the rejection of softball by some women seems to have been an early negative experience. But many softball dykes had equally bad experiences (like Missy Myers's hotbox story, for one), and here we are, still playing—or playing again, in some cases. Obviously, the reason why some dykes never got into softball is more complex, probably involving a combination of factors, including a greater susceptibility to gender-specific messages, perhaps. But the most likely explanation is that some girls have a predisposition toward physical activity and some don't.

An examination of differences within families is one of the things supporting this last assertion. Melinda Shaw, for instance, who played softball out in the dirt road in front of her house, described her family situation this way: "I was always the jock in the family, the third of four girls, and I would always try to persuade my sisters to join me in my competitive ventures, but unfortunately they were not very good at sports, thus unmotivated." In my own family, even my step-brothers were pretty much disinterested in sports, and my sister, though athletically active now, was terribly uncoordinated as a child, getting stranded in trees I had forced her to climb and breaking her thumb playing soccer. In some respects, this early dislike of sports saved my sister and other girls like her from a lot of heartache and hassle at an early age. But in other ways, they missed out on something important.

Girls And Sports: So What?

Billie Jean King: "Women have really lost out by not having sports as youngsters."[16]

Aside from the generalized discomfort and disappointment girls feel at having to (or at least feeling they have to) curb their athletic activities, what is so important about girls not getting to play team sports? It could be argued (and often has been) that sports as they are now—with their overemphasis on winning at all costs, violence, and corruption—are not something we should want to emulate or participate in any way. But in spite of their shortcomings, sports *do* have benefits. According to Barbara Fellman, a gay therapist in California, "Physical skills are imperative in the development of a positive self-image." (Research has shown that women athletes develop more desirable self-images than do nonparticipants.) "But little girls are told: 'Be careful, don't get dirty, don't get hurt.' Thus, valuable behaviors for developing self-esteem are considered masculine in our culture."[17] Extrapolating from Fellman's comment, *self-esteem* becomes defined as a masculine trait. This, in turn, may very well explain (1) why women in this society generally have such poor self-esteem and (2) one of the reasons why women are discouraged from getting involved in sports.

In addition to developing self-esteem, team sports provide a valuable opportunity for human bonding, that is, a place where people can get close to one another. Furthermore, "Men who participate in team sports are more likely to learn through sports . . . the skills, attitudes, and abilities necessary for teamwork, cooperation, and group activity. By contrast, women engage in individual, non-team, noncontact sports. As with the most accepted female roles of cohesion, teamwork and the resulting skills are not developed, encouraged, or socially approved."[18] In other words, girls are given limited access, at best, to opportunities for acquiring skills that will enable them to succeed in business or government, as well as in other areas of life where such qualities are important. Another effect of emphasizing individual sports at the expense of team sports for young girls is that it fosters a sense of isolation, giving them an early sample of how they will be pitted against one another later in life for such things as the mostly still-token positions available for women in management and academia and, in the case of straight women, for single males.

Janice Hughes: "Long ago, long before my lesbiana—I learned to value my time spent with other girls as we learned a skill together on the softball field of my little Catholic grade school deep in the heart of Texas. We learned to support each other—we learned there was Life Without Boys—and that we could grow and learn values of winning and losing together under the tutelage of another female—our coach. No matter how many laps around the bases we had to do, or how many long van trips across town we had to take, I think we all knew we were sharing something—a solidarity that we could look back on in the years ahead. We all learned to rely on Ramona's batting, Julie's catching, and our coaches' murderously strict practices to garner us victories. We learned to overlook one girl's histrionics, and another's pop flies, and to play our best."

Glenna M. Voigt: "Softball, being my first team sport, at a young age, helped me to grow up as a team player. I feel it's important that people know how to work together, to live together, to communicate, to share. By having the opportunity to do all of this at an influential age, I am able to work cooperatively in my current environment. I had a good experience growing up with softball in my life!"

Cooperation, group interaction, striving to achieve a common goal, bonding, mutual support—over and over, these were the very things women reported liking about softball, the things that drew them to softball more than any other sport. These qualities, all involving sharing and intimacy, seem that much more fitting considering that most of us began playing softball with our families— especially our fathers and brothers—and then rediscovered it later with our "sisters."

Notes

1. Dorcas Susan Butt, *Psychology of Sport: The Behavior, Motivation, Personality, and Performance of Athletes* (New York: Van Nostrand Reinhold Co., 1976), p. 68.

2. M. C. Sherriff, "The Status of Female Athletes as Viewed by Selected Peers and Parents in Certain High Schools of Central California" (Master's thesis, Chico State College, 1969), quoted in Ellen W. Gerber et al., *The American Woman in Sport* (Reading, Mass.: Addison-Wesley, 1974), pp. 362-63.

3. In "My Mother, My Rival" (*Ms.* [May 1988], pp. 88-89), Mariah Burton Nelson talks about her competitive sporting relationship from age five to adulthood with her mother. Though not about softball, Nelson's portrait is one of love of athletics and between mother and daughter.

4. Mary A. Boutilier and Lucinda SanGiovanni, *The Sporting Woman* (Champaign, Ill.: Human Kinetics Publishers, 1983), p. xii.

5. *Miller Lite Report on Women in Sports* (New York: Women's Sports Foundation, 1985), p. 3.

6. Toni McNaron, "An Interview with the Wilder Ones," *So's Your Old Lady*, no. 10 (September 1975), p. 7.

7. Rhoda Rover, "Softball: Slow Pitch, Hard Core," *Lesbian Tide* 6, no. 2 (September/October 1976): 6.

8. Betty Hicks, "Lesbian Athletes," *Christopher Street* 4, no. 3 (October/November 1979): 48.

9. This may be changing. Some of the younger women I spoke with actually got to play on Little League teams. Even so, I suspect it's still an uphill battle in that girls are not generally sought out or welcomed on these teams; they are simply tolerated.

10. Maryhel Hibben, "Dyke Softball," *Leaping Lesbian* (May 1977).

11. Boutilier and SanGiovanni, p. xii.

12. Sherriff, pp. 362-63.

13. Brenda Feigen Fasteau, "Giving Women a Sporting Chance," in *Out of the Bleachers: Writings on Women and Sports*, ed. Stephanie L. Twin (Old Westbury, N.Y.: Feminist Press, 1979), p. 167.

14. Quoted in Janice Kaplan, *Women and Sports* (New York: Viking Press, 1979), pp. 89-90.

15. Nelson, p. 89.

16. Quoted in Michele Kort, "*Ms.* Conversation," *Ms.* (February 1988), p. 60.

17. Hicks, p. 47. See also Patricia J. Murphy, "Sport and Gender," in Wilbert Marcellus Leonard II, *A Sociological Perspective of Sport*, 2d ed. (Minneapolis, Minn.: Burgess Publishing, 1984), who points out that various studies have revealed that "when women are limited in their sports participation, either by stereotypes or structural barriers, then one mechanism for feeling good, powerful, or instrumental is unavailable" (p. 201).

18. Boutilier and SanGiovanni, p. 43.

Chapter 4

Safe At Home: Softball As A Place Of Refuge

All through the winter I think about softball and worry about it and wait for it. Then in the spring I panic because I think nobody else cares about softball and we won't have a team. (Jo, The Wilder Ones)[1]

What is it about softball that inspires such passion among lesbians?

Though the aesthetics of the game—the pure physical and philosophical aspects—are certainly not without their appeal, the real attraction of softball is its social nature. What begins as cooperation and teamwork on the field often evolves into off-field intimacy and support. The many hours of practice in which we help each other to play our best, the impromptu meals afterward, the games in which we share a common goal, the celebrations and post-mortems that follow—all of these things produce a heightened sense of camaraderie among the players, a camaraderie not easily found elsewhere.

Unlike bars, for instance, in which meeting people can be a difficult and tricky business, softball is a more structured place, where other women have at least one interest in common with you. Softball also has the advantage of letting you get to know people slowly over time, and often in a healthier environment. In addition, softball is different from political and cultural organizations, which, although they have softball's structure and on-going nature, frequently have more of a class bias that discourages some women from getting involved. Such organizations may be perceived as more dangerous for women who must—or feel they must—protect their lesbian identities from becoming public. And while everything from the camaraderie to the structure of softball can also be found in other team sports, softball has a number of advantages over most of them.

First of all, softball, because of our familiarity with it and its long-standing reputation as a haven for dykes, is more universal from community to community than are other sports. A new adage for the Lesbian Nation might be: "Some communities play basketball, some play rugby, and some play soccer, but *all* lesbian communities play softball." What this means, speaking practically, is that (1) softball teams, generally being more numerous, are easier to find; (2) once you've found them, you can be pretty sure there will be other dykes on the team; and (3) most of us—even if we can't play well—at least know the basic rules of the game.

"A Good Excuse To Socialize"

Alix Dobkin: "Softball is the single greatest organizing force in lesbian society."

Miki Adachi: "This last time I got involved with softball because I just didn't want to sit at home. . . . It was a way to get out there [in the lesbian community] . . . . Actually, when I was playing softball in my earlier years, it was because I liked the game. And now, it's kind of become a social thing . . . get out there and have some fun. . . . I like being with everybody, I like the camaraderie, going out after the games. We do other things too; like we'll go to the parade or have *dim sum*. Just little things. Otherwise I might be at home."

B. Victoria: "The reason I played was to have fun. I am a lousy athlete, but when I was put on third base I got to hug everyone getting to my base!"

Pat Griffin: "It was a tradition that we [the Common Womon team] started with the Hot Flashes: whoever's home game it was planned some sort of special pre-game event. One time, they all arrived in this huge bus dressed in punk-rock outfits and made up songs and stuff. Another time, we did *Chariots Of Fire*. We all came out carrying a torch, wearing huge, white boxer shorts. But the best was—it was our home game—we decided to have this elaborate homecoming event associated with the game. And they had no idea what we were going to do. The whole league got wind that we were going to do something outrageous. So we had about sixty spectators for this game. (Usually there are only a few.) But all the people who weren't playing that night heard we were going to do something wild so everybody came to see what it was. We had a homecoming parade, starting from *way* across the field, and we had several decorated cars, and we had two queens in the back of a convertible. I got to be one of the queens. We were dressed in really outrageous old dresses from the Salvation Army. And we invited some women who used to play on our team but don't play anymore to come back as alumnae. Back in those days our motto was: 'Every dropped ball helps another woman.' So we had a banner with that on it. One of the women on the team was a majorette in high school, and she did this baton-twirling thing dressed in a lavender outfit. We had a hoop with paper on it, which the team crashed through and did forward rolls as they were introduced. And the Hot Flashes had a big hoop with paper on it that said, 'Every Common Womon needs a Hot Flash.' And they crashed through that. Then everyone lined up for the national anthem, which was 'Leaping Lesbians.' Then we played the game—the game was really anticlimactic after all of that. That same year, another two teams in the league, Womanrising and Yellow Fever—it was the year Prince Charles and Lady Di got married—had a reenactment of the royal wedding and actually played the entire game in formal prom gowns. Obviously we don't take the game as seriously as a lot of leagues do."

It is because of softball's universality and accessibility that it is a convenient focus for a variety of social activities. In fact, sometimes softball is little more than an excuse for socializing. This is certainly evident, to cite one example, in a tongue-in-cheek report of an exhibition game between the L.A. Women's Independent Softball Association's champs, the Hialeah House Sandettes, and the *Lesbian Tide* Collective, which was held "to provide an opportunity for the radical *Lesbian Tide* Collective and the Valley gay women to become better acquainted."[2]

In Chicago, the gay and lesbian Metropolitan Sports Association League is only one summer social scene, but it is definitely a major one. On Saturday and Sunday afternoons, dozens of women bring blankets, lounge chairs, coolers, suntan lotion, and snacks, then settle themselves on the sidelines to get some sun, conversation, and entertainment. Often, the ballplayers themselves will join the spectators after their games are over or on the days they don't play. There is generally a kind of party atmosphere to the whole thing. Women come with their dogs, children, lovers, friends, and even, occasionally, siblings or mothers. The convivial confusion, as much as anything, sparks a lot of interaction between those on the sidelines, making it easy to get acquainted. There are also, of course, the impromptu celebrations and parties at the bars after a game or practice.

Beyond the entertainment role softball serves once we're on a team, it also functions as a way to actually meet lesbians in the first place. This is especially true in rural areas or when one is new to a place, but can also be the case when you've lived in a city a long time and just aren't politically or culturally inclined, and either aren't interested in or aren't good at the bar scene.

New In Town?

Louise Hernandez: "About three years ago, a gay league started in San Diego. (I'm about twenty minutes north of San Diego.) I was single and I joined the league mostly for the social reason [of] meet[ing] women. So that's the only time it ever really became a social event for me. But of course, once I got in the league there was [the] competition and the activity of it. . . . I have a girlfriend now. I have a lover of fifteen months and I'm really content. I'm twenty-nine, she's thirty-three, and we're pretty set. So I'm not out to meet anybody anymore."

Berneice (from the novel *Leave A Light On For Me*): "To think if it weren't for women's rec softball, we'd never have met."[3]

Olivia: "When I first moved up to San Francisco, [softball] was an easy way for me to meet other lesbians

. . . . I had lived here for about a year or so before I came out. And when I came out, around about that time I joined the women's—the bar league, it's called here in San Francisco. It's a gay softball league. It was primarily to meet people even though I enjoy softball a lot [for its own sake]."

The main reason this strategy for meeting other lesbians works, of course, is not only that there are lesbians on those teams but also that all or most of us know this to be true. As Sandy Hayden once wrote, "I'm not saying all women who play softball are gay, but I am pointing out that if you *think* someone is gay and you don't have proof to satisfy your curiosity, [asking the question "Have you ever played softball?"] may be a solution."[4]

It's much simpler, certainly, when you know there's a specifically gay league and you know where to find it, but this knowledge applies even in so-called nongay leagues. When I moved in 1980 to Naperville, Illinois, forty miles from Chicago, where I was in a very straight corporate setting and without a car, one of the first things I did was to join a softball team. I reasoned that if there were going to be dykes out there anywhere in those 'burbs, they would be on softball teams.

The Only Game In Town

R. J.: "[Softball is] one of the only sports in a community like this where other 'family' members are. (They are so hard to find.)"

Starla Sholl: "In South Dakota, softball isn't only a sport, it's one of the only social events available for lesbians. One night a week the A league would play at the city diamonds, and the women would come from up to fifty miles to play. The league was at least 50% lesbians, although many of us believed that the other 50% either were closet cases or that they were on the verge of coming out. On Tuesday nights, even the few women who didn't play softball came out, and we all would sit on the same bleachers. Some people may have guessed we were lesbians, but in that area most people don't even know what the word means. Sitting on the same bleachers, on Tuesday nights, was one of the best ways to really feel the solidarity of the South Dakota dykes . . .especially since there are so few 'blatant' events."

Sometimes the difficulty of finding other dykes is not just a function of having recently relocated. In rural areas, lesbians tend to be scattered over a lot of acreage, and there are generally few places to socialize—bars, coffeehouses, and women's bookstores being most conspicuous by their absence. Both the scattering and the lack of places to gather make it problematic for lesbians to meet each other and to locate places to mingle once they've become acquainted. For rural lesbians, the game of softball functions today much as it did thirty or forty years ago: as a singularly safe place to meet lesbians. As R. J. has said, "It's very important *not* to be identified [as a lesbian] in this part of the country."

Given that softball is also one of the few activities available to straight women in rural areas, it provides a safe cover for lesbians interested in hanging out together. Sometimes the straight women on the team know who the lesbians are, but most often they don't. In either case, lesbians seem to have a second sense—a sort of radar—that lets us pick each other out.

A Healthy Alternative

Laurie: "I use sports as a whole to meet people—I rarely ever go to bars for that purpose. If I do go to a bar, it is to socialize with the friends I have met through sports. Team sports are the main social outlets in my life. I depend on them for emotional support, physical activity, a sense of belonging, a comfortable atmosphere, and an outlet for my competitive nature."

Fran: "I met my first lover through softball. . . . I think softball is a good place to meet people and probably always will be—especially for the young people who can't go to the bar or anything. My daughter—she's eighteen—she plays softball. She has a girlfriend, too. They met playing softball in high school together."

Linda Locke: "I was adopted; my parents are white [and I am Korean]. So I grew up kind of isolated from a lot of Asian women. The interesting thing is, the softball teams that I've played on up here are Asian teams. So for me, it was a way of meeting Asian women and a way that felt real comfortable, more than, say, at that point, a political meeting or an organization like that. So what happened is I met them in a way that I felt real comfortable and then after that I could go and meet with Asian women on another level. Because [in the beginning] I felt like maybe I didn't have that 'Asian experience.'. . . It was a way. . . to feel like I was part of the group. . . . It's like a way of coming home in a sense."

Valerie Edwards: "There are so few places for women to go and meet apart from bars. And unless you're interested in getting involved in a political organization, it's very difficult to meet lesbians. . . . It is an ideal way to get to know other people."[5]

Although larger towns and cities may provide more opportunities for socializing than there are out in the countryside, those opportunities are not always suitable for everyone. By way of example, for women who have a problem with alcohol, or who don't like to dance, or who have allergies to cigarette smoke, or who can't or don't want to stay up late, or who are not adept at handling unstructured social situations, bars are not a viable place to socialize. Janice Kaplan quotes one woman, a writer and fitness consultant in San Francisco, who thinks "sports are replacing bars as a way to meet people."[6]

Also, for women who are closeted, lesbian political and cultural activism can be too public and, therefore, too risky. And some women just aren't interested in activism of any kind.

Even for women who *do* enjoy going to bars or who *are* involved culturally or politically, softball can be an important—even necessary—change of pace. Compared to the often surreal feeling of bar life and the serious quality of activism, softball can be a mental health-saving escape, something relaxing and *fun*. I know it's been a lifesaver for me.

When I moved from the suburbs into Chicago, knowing how lousy I am at getting acquainted with people in bars, I joined practically everything I heard of: the local chapter of the Feminist Writers' Guild, a literary magazine collective, the staff of the women's bookstore, and a group engaged in founding a journal devoted to women's music and culture.[7]

I was very active in our lesbian culture and, not insignificantly, I was quite successful in building up a large circle of friends and acquaintances. My cultural activities were gratifying on two levels: mentally and emotionally. But I started to feel burnt out after a couple of years and realized there was still one major void in my life: the physical.

It's not that I hadn't tried to find both softball and volleyball teams here in Chicago. I had. But I hadn't heard about our gay sports organization (clearly a gap in the knowledge of my literary/political friends!), and all of the park rec leagues here play a weird brand of softball known only to Chicagoans. It's called "sixteen inch" because it is played with a ball that has a sixteen-inch diameter, and it is played without a glove. I tried it once, but found that, not being able to get my hand around the ball (which is about the size of a cantaloupe), throwing it was something akin to putting the shot—and all of the stories about broken fingers didn't exactly sell the game to me either.

Luckily, around the same time I was experiencing burnout, I discovered the Gay Athletic Association (as it was called in 1984), and that it had a women's twelve-inch softball league. Softball has been an important social and recreational outlet for me since then. Not only does it provide me with much-needed exercise and give me a break from intense cerebral activity, but it has provided me with an important "home base" as well. While my literary friends are without a doubt very significant in my life, there is something special about the bonds I have formed with my softball buddies, a closeness and ease of relating that I've seldom found elsewhere.

We Are Family

Mary Farmer: "I enjoy the camaraderie, I enjoy the teamwork, and all the social stuff that comes from it. Our softball team is really like an extended family and has been for a long time. It's a great source of pride to

me and to my teammates. It's one of the most important things I do in my life."

Meryl Moskowitz: "When I change from my business
suit into my sweatsuit and head for the ball field, I'm
home again! My team is my 'family,' and though I don't
see them all year round, we always are concerned and
in touch."

Pat Griffin: "Several years ago. . ., we *were* a family.
We were a very close-knit group. [But] some people have
left the area, and the team has sort of changed character over the years. The summer before last we had one
of our *worst* seasons—not necessarily in terms of wins
and losses, but it just seemed like the team had no
heart. There were really serious questions about
whether or not there was enough of a core of us to keep
it going, that we would have a team. So we had a big
meeting in spring to kick off the next season and to
figure out what was wrong. What we realized is that,
those of us who had been on the team a long time, we
were sort of imposing on the new women this *family*
thing from the past. And they resented that. They
didn't want to be like the team was [before]. They
wanted to be whatever they were. So those of us who
had been around a long time just had to let go of that,
and once we did, as it turned out this past summer, not
only did we have our very best season playing-wise, but
we also just had a really good time. It was not the same
and it never will be, but we created something else that
was terrific. So there is definitely a sense of extended
family to the Common Womon team."

M.: "Softball makes my summer fun. I'm with very
close friends with whom I can. . .share some B.S. and

CITY PARK: MARCH SUNDAY

They gather slowly; it is the first
time this year for some, the first time
in twenty years for others.
Tossing balls in high arcs, bringing
beagles on chains, sharing banana splits
from Baskin-Robbins, their numbers
increase. Now, small boys and fathers
must be removed diplomatically
from the diamond. Wooden bats
smack together between the plops
dropping into leather pockets.

An audience of kites collects,
quarrels overhead. Ones and twos,
counted off, the teams form:
twos take the field. Third base,
whose hand was minced by a vegetable
grinder earlier in the week, cannot
wear a glove. Center field and second
huddle together, jackets flapping,
lighting cigarettes. The catcher hunts
for home plate. The pitcher smooths the mound
with bare feet.

Batters take the plate: some swing
like limbs in the Kansas wind, back
and forth, in a rustle of words;
for others, balls scurry through
the dirt, over frantic hands and feet;
some sail it kite-high, off toward
the Safeway, then watch a glove
hug it close. Dust blows
applause in the face of the next batter
who swings, looks straight
at the gold medal of sun, starts
to run as the runner comes home.

(From *Each Hand A Map* by Anita Skeen, Naiad Press, 1986.)

beers. I don't play [softball] to find lovers but to be with loving friends."

R. J.: "When I was in my early teens (fifteen or sixteen) and still coming to grips with my own lesbianism, feeling very alone and confused—I got on a [softball] team in Billings, Montana, with a female coach—probably twenty-five years old or so. I think now she knew what I was going through and she taught me more about the game and myself than anyone else I've ever met. Because of . . . her and the other team members, [I felt] like I did belong."

Mariah Burton Nelson, an associate editor of *Women's Sports and Fitness*, has observed that "women writers are examining not only the traditional lessons that sport offers: teamwork, leadership, enjoyment—but also less traditional lessons of sport: commitment, intimacy, bonding with others of the same gender."[8] If that is indeed true, it is probably because those "less traditional lessons" are often some of the most important aspects—for women—of sports.

For many women, in fact, this sense of intimacy and bonding runs very deep—*extended family* was a phrase I heard with some regularity. And the sponsor and manager of one of the teams here in Chicago is frequently heard referring to the women on her team as "her kids."

Like most families, while we don't do *everything* together, we do share a lot: going on picnics, celebrating our birthdays, going to concerts and movies in groups of four or six, inviting each other over or out to dinner, helping one another move, and playing other sports and games together. And also like most families, we do more than just have good times. We help take care of each other when we're sick or injured, and we comfort each other in times of loss. Sometimes, as R. J.'s story illustrates, we even help each other deal with issues surrounding our lesbianism.

Caring: Never Out Of Season

In the South and in much of California, the weather permits softball playing almost all year round. In places like Chicago, where summer is short, our season has a distinct beginning and end. But the season's close doesn't necessarily signal the end of the close relationships we form.

No family is perfect, however, and even the most close-knit teams have their problems: couples breaking up, "sibling rivalry" for prized positions on the field, misunderstandings, hurt feelings, gossip. Frequently, our fondness for one another is greater than whatever the problem is, and we are able to resolve things. Occasionally something will happen that causes irreparable damage, however, and there is a rupture in the family, a time of great sadness—and sometimes bitterness. Even then, women seldom quit softball. When things don't work out on one team, they leave to join another, or help to form a new team and, ultimately, a new family—even if that's not what they initially planned. There's just something about softball . . . .

Notes

1. Toni McNaron, "An Interview with the Wilder Ones," *So's Your Old Lady*, no. 10 (September 1975), p. 8.

2. "Sandettes Blast Tide," *Lesbian Tide* 3, no. 4 (November 1973): 24. See also Pat Greene, "Beautiful Women's Softball," *Lesbian Tide* 2, no. 12 (July 1973): 3, which reports on another game that was accompanied by a picnic and a variety of other social activities.

3. Jean Swallow, *Leave A Light On For Me* (San Francisco: Spinsters/Aunt Lute, 1986), p. 2. Oddly enough, as central as the role of softball is in the lesbian community. *Leave A Light On For Me* is the first lesbian book in which softball figures prominently. The only other women's softball novels that I know of (Sara Vogan, *In Shelly's Leg* [St. Paul, Minn.: Graywolf Press, 1985]; and Ellen Cooney, *All The Way Home* [New York: G. P. Putnam's Sons, 1984]) are very heterosexual, though the feelings of camaraderie and community, so evident in lesbian softball, are also present in these novels.

4. Sandy Hayden, "Giving Her Away," *Focus* (May/June 1980), p. 24.

5. Valerie Edwards, "Notso Amazons Not So Competitive Softball," *Everywoman's Almanac 1987* (Toronto, 1987).

6. Janice Kaplan, *Women and Sports* (New York: Viking Press, 1979), p. 79. See also Linn ni Cobhan, "Lesbians in Physical Education and Sport" in *Lesbian Studies: Present and Future*, ed. Margaret Cruikshank (Old Westbury, N.Y.: Feminist Press, 1982), who suggests that athletes may not need bars, dances, or meetings to form their social communities among women because they form their own social groups. Characteristically, a male sports psychologist, Bruce Ogilivie (quoted in C. W. Nevius, "Theories on Homosexuality in Sports," *San Francisco Chronicle* May 14, [1981]) "calls female athletes 'cultural mutants,' because 'they defied the culture they live in.' It is no surprise, Ogilivie says, to find these alienated women turning to each other for support." While there is little doubt that both athleticism and lesbianism can be alienating factors in a woman's life that encourage the formation of bonds between and among softball dykes, most women tend to focus less on such negative aspects and more on the cooperation, shared energy, and mutual support they find in softball.

7. The journal I cofounded, along with Toni Armstrong, Jr., Michele Gautreaux, and Ann Morris, is *Hot Wire: A Journal of Women's Music and Culture*, a nationally (and internationally) distributed periodical, and the only one of its kind. I am no longer on *Hot Wire*'s staff, but I contributed an article on the All-American Girls Professional Baseball League in 1987.

8. Mariah Burton Nelson, foreword in *More Golden Apples*, ed. Sandra Martz (Manhattan Beach, Calif.: Papier-Mache Press, 1986), p. iii.

Chapter 5

The Double Play (Or, Love On The Softball Field)

Child psychologist Jean Piaget found that in childhood games boys are more concerned with the rules, while girls are more concerned with the relationships among the players, even if the game suffers in the process.[1]

If the word *girls* were replaced by the word *lesbians* in the second half of the quotation above, there would be little doubt about the name of the game: dyke softball.

Lesbian folk singer Alix Dobkin, who plays softball in Woodstock, New York, says that lesbians don't care nearly as much about winning as they do about the relationships between the women on the team. Though not all lesbians are more invested in relationships than in the game, if you look at any softball team that dykes play on, two or more of the women are bound to be—or have been—involved with one another.

It's not so much that lesbians play softball expressly for the sake of forming relationships, though certainly a few do. It's more that, when the women *do* begin playing, relationships form naturally: "To play sports with women is to love women, to be passionate about women, to be intimate with women."[2] Once those relationships have formed, they can become more important than the game itself. And when that happens, playing dyke softball is like walking through a minefield, with its fluctuating relation-ships—forming, ending, changing right before your eyes.

But what is it that makes these relationships so perva-sive? What happens when lovers on a team split up? What are the effects on the team? How are *softball* dykes simi-lar and dissimilar to other groups of women in this re-spect?

In The Beginning, There Was Love

Joan Bender: "My last lover—we knew each other be-fore we played on the same team but we weren't close, and now we are together as a result of softball cuz we got to know each other. . . ."

Missy Myers: "[I] have. . . shared the diamond, at one time or another, with all but one of my lovers."

Linda Locke: "Most of the women I've been involved with, I met them through sports. I go to bars to go danc-ing, but I don't meet my lovers or my friends in bars; I meet them through sports."

A Conversation With Erin And Jody: Part 1

Yvonne: What role did softball play in getting you to-gether?

Erin: Well, we had practices and then all went out for dinner after.

Jody: It was O.K. for us to discuss softball things. Like (we were talking about this the other day) that out on the diamond we had great eye contact and were very comfortable with each other. Because we had a shared experience and we were good! And we

WANDA, SMITTEN WITH THE SECOND BASEWOMAN, DISGRACES HER TEAM BY FORGETTING TO RUN.

knew softball. We had this whole relationship on the field between the shortstop and third baseman. Don't you think that was true?

Erin: Yeah.

Jody: Where it was O.K. And then Erin was saying the minute we walked across the third base line, back toward "the fans," it would stop. It was O.K. to be demonstrative on the field, to slap each other['s hand] or hug each other or something like that. And have eye contact. And laugh. And really crack ourselves up. But the minute we walked across the third base line, it wasn't O.K. I think that's accurate, don't you?

Erin: Right.

Yvonne: What if you'd played different positions? What if you hadn't been playing right next to each other? Would that have changed anything?

Jody: If I had played infield, I don't think it would've changed anything. I don't think it would've mattered.

Erin: Where you were playing?

Jody: Yeah. When I was playing first base at practices I flirted with her; I would've flirted with her at second base; I would've flirted with her at short center. [Pause.] I would've.

Erin: You didn't flirt with me at first.

Jody: At first? I always did. I dazzled you with my performance. I smiled every time you got the ball to me. You don't remember that, do you? I hotdogged. I did everything.

Erin: Well, I thought you were just good. I didn't know you were hotdogging.

Yvonne: What about you, Erin?

Erin: Well, I know that in the last game when Jody played short center instead of third base and was standing behind me, it really made a difference in my performance. [She laughs.]

Yvonne: How so?

Erin: I couldn't concentrate. Because I was wondering if my shirt was tucked in right or my shorts were too short or hanging down too long or if I was too sweaty or too dirty.

Jody: So then one time I walked off the field and I asked Erin, "What do you look at when you're concentrating on the field?"

Erin: That's when you were playing third.

Jody: "Do you look at the batter and wait for the ball to come to you? Or do you follow the ball from pitcher to batter?" And she didn't have an immediate answer, which kind of shocked me. But then she tells me later what she's been looking at.

Yvonne: What *had* she been looking at?

Erin: Every time she got ready for the pitch . . . she'd like, get her toes placed into the dirt and swing around like this and get her cleats into the dirt. And while she was doing this her butt and her whole body would move around when she would do this.

Jody: She was watching me!

Erin: I was watching her get set, waiting for the ball. So I never really used to watch when [the pitcher] released the pitch. I kind of . . . I would always catch [sight of] the pitch when it was about five feet from the batter. And not really pay attention to the ball before that because I was watching Jody get set.

Yvonne: Did playing softball have any other significant impact on the development of your relationship?

Erin: I think the way a person plays softball has a way of showing you what they're really like inside, emotionally. And their strengths and weaknesses. And how much they believe in themselves.

Yvonne: So softball kind of speeded up the process of getting to know each other.

Erin: Yeah. Yeah. What their expectations are . . .

Jody: It didn't speed up the process for me. But it satisfied my attraction to Erin.

Yvonne: You felt like you hadn't been mistaken in your attraction . . .

Jody: Right. And you know, she was involved with somebody else. So what it did was, it acted like a substitute for my satisfaction.

Yvonne: So you could feel . . . .

Jody: It was a shared experience.

Yvonne: You could sort of transfer your feelings for Erin as a person to Erin as a softball player. You could admire her as a softball player.

Jody: Because I wasn't able to get to know Erin, as a person, intimately. I was able to enjoy admiring her as a softball player, and I could be satisfied with the closeness we had during softball.

Anyone who has ever had any real contact with softball dykes knows exactly how prevalent the occurrence of "love on the softball field" is. But why is this so?

The things that make each of our teams into an extended family are the same things that create an environment encouraging other kinds of intimacy as well. The long hours together, practicing and playing; the shared experiences; an atmosphere allowing for few pretenses; the general camaraderie; a tradition of support and encouragement—all of these things make softball fertile ground for attractions, infatuations, and romance. In addition, while athletic lesbians tend to find other athletic women attractive, they also pick up clues about the other's private personality in her public approach to the game and her performance on the field. As Mariah Burton Nelson has said, "Competition is about passion for perfection, and passion for other people who join in this impossible quest. What better way to get to know someone than to test your abilities together, to be daring and sweaty and exhausted together?"[3]

For jocks, a woman's athletic ability is a major point of attraction. I don't know *how* many times I've heard things like, "She's not only cute, but she's an excellent shortstop." There is something very appealing—to athletic women, anyway—about a woman who has good control of her body, whose muscles are toned and firm, and who has a grasp of the game in all its subtleties.

P.L.: "[Softball takes] a lot of time. . . . It's difficult for people who aren't involved in softball together (or sports together) to be involved [with one another]. You could possibly be on another team, but. . .with the

amount of time you get to spend with each other—
some people just resent it."

Yet another reason softball dykes tend to bond to one another is that they understand each other's passion for the
game. Women who aren't themselves participants on a
team often find their patience and understanding strained
with their ball-playing lovers. There are the one or two
nights set aside for practice, plus an additional day or two
a week for games (which often take precedence over any
other plans), plus there are the hours of ritual socializing
spent with teammates, and so on. Even women with the
best of intentions for letting their lovers do their own thing
find themselves getting angry after the sixth or seventh
time they hear, "The game ran late," or, "I just went to
have a beer with the team."

While it is an accepted truism that it is healthy for couples to have separate interests, and while having a lover
who doesn't play softball may keep your relationship safe
from the vagaries of summer softball romances, being involved with a woman immune to your all-consuming at-
tachment to the game and to a jovial set of teammates can
put an undue strain on the relationship. I've known several
women who are softball dykes whose lovers aren't. And
most of them have found themselves in situations, at one
time or another, such as these:

> •Sarah wanted to go celebrate their unexpected vic-
> tory with the rest of her team but couldn't because
> her lover Jean was waiting for her at home.
> •Liz was angry with Joan because she couldn't get
> Joan to skip her Saturday game so they could spend
> a romantic weekend alone together.
> •Lisa complained that she hardly ever got to see
> Sue anymore, now that softball season had started.

PERFECT NIGHT

The jock is dressed in wool tonight
She's got a baseball glove, a cap tonight
There's a competitive look in her eyes in spite of her generous heart
And she'll play ball with her true love
Take in a home run or two
And nothing short of a perfect night will do.

(From "Perfect Night" by Holly Near on *Lifeline*, Holly Near and Ronnie Gilbert, produced by Redwood Records, RR404.)

•Jennifer couldn't help being jealous of all the congratulatory and sympathetic hugs between her lover Vicki, at first base, and the woman who played second base. What was *really* going on at all those Tuesday night practices?

Even though problems like these aren't insurmountable, and softball romances have problems of their own, many jocks find much more understanding partners—at least concerning time devoted to softball—in their sister jocks.

And When Love Dies?
It's A Family Affair

While love is a personal and private thing, its demise often has a way of becoming very public. And just as divorce in heterosexual marriages tears families apart, so the end of relationships between two softball dyke teammates tears teams—and extended families—apart.

P. L.: "It was during the season [when we split up]. It was real quiet—no one on the team talked to me about anything that was going on. They basically rallied a-

round her more, I would say. I still played with them, but there wasn't that team unity anymore. . . . I think it brought our team down as a whole because there wasn't that unity. . . . I didn't think those people were my friends anymore. . . . Then when football started after softball, I didn't get any contact about that at all. And then when I *was* contacted, they were like, well you can't bring your girlfriend—my new girlfriend—but [my ex's new girlfriend] was playing all the time, so . . . . [But] they're starting to come around more and more now. . . . They called about playing softball this year. . . and they said, 'Go ahead and bring [your new girlfriend].' So [playing on a new team this year] was basically my own choice because I didn't want to get involved in conflict at all. I just wanted to play softball."

Pat Parker: "For a lot of younger women, the team—it *is* their social life; it is their cruising place. So I've watched different couples change identities. One of the hardest parts of coaching, for me, is to teach these people not to quite bring it all on the field with them. Because when you look up and your right fielder is standing in right field with tears streaming down her face, you know you're in a world of trouble. She's not thinking about softball right now."

Olivia: "I was coaching the team. And the two [other] people involved were playing on the team. It's difficult to say how it affected my coaching. It was a situation where I tried not to deal with that on the field. And I think it was easier for me than the people who had to play because they had to actually perform. . . . Then one would refuse to come when the other was there. Basically the team fell apart, is what happened. It was just too hard for everybody. . . . People were pretty good about not taking sides and stuff, but it was difficult for people to continue to play together."

Mo: "[It] seems that some have a harder time forgetting their personal soap operas, which impairs their ability to do and act for the good of the team. They can't forget themselves, be objective, and not let outside emotional problems affect their attitude."

Celeste Methot: "It was tragic. There was one incident where my team was playing the national tournament in Atlanta—well actually Marietta. And there were these two women who had kind of been off and on all season but were really more on than off, and I played social worker for the two of them. I was always trying to patch them up, and they both always came running to me for comfort. And we were in the national tournament and were doing really well. We were playing in a game on Sunday morning, at like nine o'clock. They had, for some unknown reason, gone out the night before and had a *huge* fight. And both of them happened to have a large role on our team; they played key roles. And one of them just did not show up for the start of the game. And when she finally got there, she was half-drunk and incapable of playing. It got the team so pissed because she did not care enough to remain sober or be there on time for that game that was very important to us. We ended up getting fourteenth place instead of what could've been third or fourth place."

Miki Adachi: "I was the coach. And I got involved with a player. In fact I had a rule before the season not to do that and I broke it. I think even the best laid plans go astray. Good intentions but it just didn't work . . . .

We're still friends though. We were mature enough to get through it."

A Conversation With Erin And Jody: Part 2

> Yvonne: Have you thought about what would happen if you split up, what that would do? Would you continue playing on the same team? Would you have any problems with that?
>
> Jody: I would have to play on another team. It would be too difficult for me, initially. It would just be too painful.
>
> Erin: I think it depends on the depth of the relationship and the emotional involvement.
>
> Jody: I guess what I'm saying is, it's deep, for me. So it would be too painful at first. Not that I couldn't come back around, too. But I would need some distance. Because that was one of my initial satisfactions and attractions—is how you play ball.
>
> Yvonne: How about you, Erin?
>
> Erin: I'd probably move out of state. [Laughter.] Yep. I wouldn't even play in the same league. I wouldn't even watch the games. . . . [Because] this is a good one. This is a good one.
>
> Jody: The question is? Or the relationship?
>
> Erin and Yvonne: The relationship.

A Kaleidoscope Of Couples

Kate Clinton: "The shortstop of my team isn't talking to the pitcher because they're sleeping with the same woman who is the catcher."

Florence: "I have seen, in many cases, where if lovers are playing on the same team and they split up, one of them will leave the team for whatever reason. And it can be a problem keeping a good team together because a lot of them, although they're good, they haven't learned to separate their playing ability and purpose from their love life. . . . It's sort of hard to keep the unity there when you have a lot of personal things that become involved."

J. T.: "What I find fascinating about 'love on the softball field' is, at the end of the season, *everybody* has rearranged."

Judy Thompson: "I enjoy straight leagues much more . . . because you don't have somebody whining that their girlfriend's out fooling around with somebody else, 'I can't show up because this one's showing up.' . . . I coach a team and each year it's like, O.K., who's with who, and who do I get to ask back? And who can't come back because their lover broke up with them? It's just headache after headache."

Each year teams go through everything from minor changes in personnel to major upheavals as couples rearrange and re-form. Not all changes in personnel, of course, are due to matters related to love—sometimes there are just differences of opinion or in philosophy of play, personality conflicts, changing allegiances, and so on. But most teams regularly add and subtract people as women bring their new lovers to the team, as one half of a former couple leaves—sometimes two or three others leaving with her in a show of support—and so on. Rivalries spring up between teams on which ex-lovers are playing. Occasionally, women are able to resolve their differences between seasons (or over the years), and it's not uncommon to find a woman with a lover and an ex-lover or two playing on the same team. On my team, for example, the pitcher is my ex-lover. And she, in turn, has another ex-lover besides me on the team, and I can think of at least three other sets of ex's—four, if you count the two women who were together a few years ago, split up, and are back together.

In part, this "in-breeding" has to do with the fact that for many women, softball (and other team sports), constitutes their primary social network: softball is where they hang out, where they meet others. When one relationship ends, therefore, the two women often meet their new romantic interests in this same setting.

The whole pattern of coupling, uncoupling, and recoupling—along with all its effects on the team—is one of the things that sets openly lesbian teams apart from straight teams and from partly lesbian-but-closeted teams. On straight teams, when women break up with their boyfriends, though *their* performance on the field might be impaired, it generally doesn't have an impact on the rest of the team. Unless, of course, the boyfriend is also the coach, who is now dating another woman on the team. But the odds of that happening just aren't stacked as precariously as they are on all-lesbian teams with lesbian coaches. And on teams where there are some dykes in among the straight women but the dykes are mostly closeted, a breakup seldom affects the team as a whole because the women involved have chosen not to be (or can't be) open about the relationship they had in the first place. Though the human drama of shifting couples on lesbian teams can be nerve-racking, it seems to me part of being a member of a family—taking the bad stuff with the good is the price one has to pay for intimacy.

Though this shifting landscape of partners may set us apart from straight or closeted teams, it is not at all dissimilar from what happens in other parts of the lesbian community.

Stephie: "[Splitting up] is really hard on friends who know them and on each other because [of] who's saying what about whom—'Oh, I don't want to play if she's going to be there'; 'Her new girlfriend's there'—it's the same stuff. It's just like the bars."

The almost incestuous nature of lesbian relationships occurs because we are a tight-knit community (especially within our subcommunities) with certain limitations on our socializing. It's hard not to get involved with someone who doesn't have some prior connection—no matter how tenuous—to you or someone else in your life. That's something that's true whether you're a political activist, a bar dyke, or a jock.

But for all love's ups and downs, despite the complications that can arise, and even though most of us now and then forswear love, we seldom actually turn down an opportunity for "true love" when it comes our way—even and especially on the softball field. Because you just never know. . . . As Joan Bender of Rapid City, South Dakota, says, "If [my lover and I] hadn't played ball together, we wouldn't be together now."

Notes

1. Letty Cottin Pogrebin, *Among Friends* (New York: McGraw-Hill Book Co., 1987), p. 281.

2. Mariah Burton Nelson, "My Mother, My Rival," *Ms.* (May 1988), pp. 88-89, esp. 89. Nelson astutely finishes her observation by saying, "How scary. Or, depending on your point of view, how thrilling," citing this as one reason some women "have an ambivalent, if not downright hostile attitude toward sports" (p. 89).

3. Nelson, p. 88.

Chapter 6

The Pitch:
The Aesthetics
Of Dyke Softball,
Inside And Out

Recently, I watched a group of young athletes perform a dance choreographed by Abner Doubleday. I
admire the courageous grace of women softball
players. (Betty Hicks)[1]

For the athletically uninvolved, it might seem as likely
for aesthetics and softball to be linked as it would for the
pairing of champagne and peanut butter. But to avid softball players and spectators alike, there is indeed a beauty
to softball. There are the sheer physical aspects of the game
—the sights, sounds, smells—that trigger pleasurable memories of games past or signal excellence of performance
for the players. There is the thrill of a well-executed play,
the mystique of so many different parts coming together
to form a coherent whole, and a variety of other, less tan-
gible factors for both players and spectators.

In addition to the physical aspects of the game, many
of the qualities that seem integral to softball—the camaraderie, cooperation, mutual support, and sharing—are
what attract us mentally and emotionally to the game.
The extent and way in which these qualities are present
is in large part determined by the team's, and its players',

philosophies on competition. Who gets to play, who makes the coaching decisions, how important is winning—these considerations affect not only the aesthetic qualities of the game for each of the players, but also what we see on the field. On an even deeper level, there are the images of ourselves as female athletes that we carry around, influencing both what we get out of softball and what we are willing to put into it.

Softball And The Five Senses
Hearing

•There is something deeply satisfying about the sound of a ball being hit—not down near the handle, but squarely, at the fat part of the bat.

•"Of all the sounds of summer, I think one of my favorites is that made when a softball hits cleanly into a glove." (Toni McNaron)[2]

•If it weren't for the shouts of encouragement from one's teammates, the batter's box might be one of the loneliest places there is.

•Nancy C. cites two of her favorite sounds as the clank of the metal bats as they drop to the ground together ("Like chimes," I interject) and the click of cleats across the parking lot as she approaches the field.

•Click.
Click.
Click.
My spikes took our dugout steps one at a time, careful not to slip on damp concrete. No point breaking a leg the first day of practice.
Clickity, clickity, clickity.

New season, new shoes—nickel spikes and white kid leather. Best pair in the Wilson sports catalog. (R. R. Knudson, *Zanboomer*)[3]

•The sound of praise from one's sister teammates, from the fans, and sometimes even from the opposing team make the best played ball even sweeter.

Taste

•Certain beverages, otherwise perfectly ordinary, can taste particularly refreshing during, or after, a long softball game out in the summer sun: Gatorade, ice water, beer. In Chicago's Metropolitan Sports Association (MSA) league, another taste we look forward to every summer is the steak tacos sold from the mobile taco stand that comes to rest every Saturday and Sunday morning along the baselines of two fields.

•The simple act of licking your lips can yield the ocean and its salt-sea air.

•A daring slide on a wind-blown dusty field may leave you with the dry taste of grit or dirt in your mouth. Though not generally considered a pleasant taste, it can evoke the pleasure of the whole softball experience. And with dirt in your mouth, it is hard to deny you are in the game.

Touch

•One of my favorite tactile experiences in softball is the feel of the thin leather skin that is my batting glove as it envelops my hand.

•Also pleasant is the subtle weight of the baseball mitt at the end of one's arm, which begins to feel so natural, you forget the mitt is there. There have been days when I was startled to look down and see my skinny brown wrist sticking out of a big webbed hand.

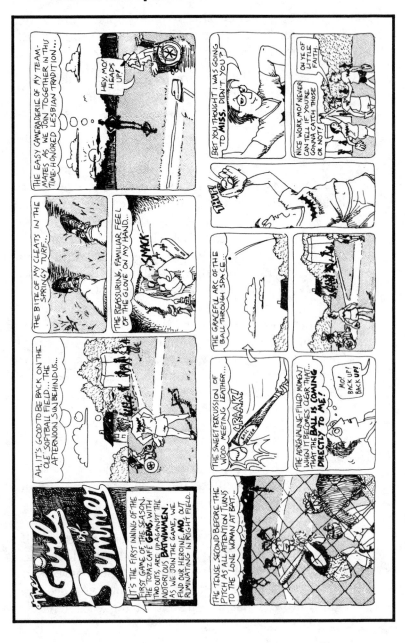

Though it looked strange, it *felt* like part of me. Gloves become, over time, molded to fit our hands and are like old friends. We mourn their passing.

•I like the feel of my fingers wrapped around the narrow bat handle and the tension in my arms when bat and ball connect.

•Cleats gripping the dirt give one a sure-footedness that radiates out into an overall confidence.

•J. T. talks about the special feeling of nervous excitement she gets in the pit of her stomach as she stands in the batter's box.

•One of the few times that a film of sweat can feel good is during a softball game. It is evidence of hard work, of working "bad" things out of one's system, of living fully. There is also the contradictory feel of the sun baking the sweat in and drawing it out.

•There is the way your lungs expand to fill your chest when you turn a good play.

Smell

Although the sense of smell probably plays a lesser role in softball than the other senses do, or than it might in an indoor sport, there are still certain smells that softball players enjoy.

•Probably the most cherished smell of softball players is that of glove leather.

•Other favorites might be freshly cut grass and damp earth.

•Human smells are also important—especially with all the hugging that tends to go on at lesbian games—smells like sun-warmed skin, suntan lotion, and sweat.

•Depending on where you live and play ball, the fresh, out-of-doors air may be a smell you associate with softball. In Chicago, the MSA games are played on fields that lie between an eight-lane thoroughfare and Lake Michigan, so that our fresh air is often intermingled with car exhaust and alewives.

Sight

Anyone who says that softball is a boring game to watch isn't looking at the right things.

•There are the women ballplayers: the diversity of size, shape, and color; muscles glistening with sweat; the obvious confidence and the ease with which they own their bodies; the fluid motions—snagging a wildly bouncing ball with a mitt, scooping the ball out of the glove with a free hand, and throwing it sharply and well to a teammate, as if this were all one motion; their grace as they bound across the field, then dive to snatch the ball from flight at the last moment, rolling to break their fall and leaping to their feet, glove and ball held triumphantly high; the fierce determination in their faces as they hit the ball or run the bases.

•There is the majestic arc of a ball in flight across a soft blue summer sky, or the vague blur of a ball sharply hit.

•J. T. speaks almost wistfully of the little puffs of dirt that rise in the infield when a ball scuds across it or when a player slides into a bag.

•For pure visual images, you can't beat softball: the symmetry of the baselines, like two outspread arms, and the bases themselves, echoing each other within the lines; the crisp color contrasts of the dirt-brown base paths, the green infield and outfield, and the white bases and lines; and the pleasant, sometimes vibrant, repetition of color in the uniforms among the members of each team.

It's How You Play The Game

Whether the game is a well-choreographed dance, a comedy of errors, a heart-warming drama, an uplifting experience, a valiant effort, or a study in frustration, a team's philosophy is instrumental in shaping the experience. Sometimes this philosophy is spoken, sometimes not. Sometimes a philosophy is controlled by the coach, sometimes by the team as a whole (and the dynamics of who does the controlling can themselves be telling). Team philosophies determine who plays and/or who doesn't; who coaches and how; the frequency of and the way that practices are conducted; the tone of the game; the interaction among a team's players as well as their interactions with other teams; the quality of ball being played; and, no doubt, a number of other things we aren't even aware of. Some team philosophies are patterned after male models of competition, while others call the traditional ethics of competition into question. Philosophies range from "winning is everything," to "playing one's best is what counts," to "having fun is all that matters"—and a myriad of combinations.

But whatever their philosophy, lesbian teams unavoidably take on a character that makes them distinct from men's teams. While women's teams can sometimes be just as aggressive and relentless in their pursuit of excellence as men's teams, most women seem to know how to mix a competitive spirit with sensitivity to others' feelings. (Some might argue there is *too* much sensitivity on lesbian teams!) As the respondents to the Miller Lite survey on women in sports agreed, "Women have something to teach men about humane competition."[4]

Feminist Softball?—Three Stories

In *The Sporting Woman*, Mary Boutilier and Lucinda SanGiovanni make a number of astute observations about the current and future status of women and sports. Among these observations are those that question the structure of sports. Usually the definition of sports accepts the competitive framework as a given, and the standard question is whether women are capable of participating. "The question posed is how women will adjust to the potential conflict sports activities may engender. The feeling seems to be that since they are the ones who want to enter the Sports-World it is they, not sport, who will have to change." But as Boutilier and SanGiovanni point out, "Sport, as presently constructed, fails to reflect those interests and

---

WHAT'S IN A NAME

A team's name reflects the personality of the team. Some teams are no-nonsense and simply adopt their sponsor's name as their own. Other teams are more focused on camaraderie, such as Kindred Spirits, in Chicago, or on a feminist consciousness, such as the Common Womon team in the Northampton-Amherst area of Massachusetts. Still other teamnames reflect a sense of humor— perhaps, even, a propensity for downplaying the seriousness of the competition. While a team's name doesn't necessarily have anything to do with how well they do or don't play or with their overall character, I must confess to a certain predisposition toward the clever. Here are a few of my favorites—past, present, and fictional.

The Wildcat Strikes (San Francisco)
Pray for Rain (Chicago)
Batwimmin (Alison Bechdel, *Dykes To Watch Out For*)
Diamond Cutters (Naperville, Illinois)
Lickity Splits (Toronto)
Juicyfruits (Toronto)
Bluegays (Toronto)
Bats Out of Hell (Lucy Moynihan, Chicago)

values that are central to women's world-view and life experience."[5]

The stories that follow not only illustrate this but also show genuine effort *to change sports so that they do reflect women's lives.*

Pat Griffin And The Tri-County League
Northampton-Amherst Area, Massachusetts

"We try to define what we do as 'feminist softball,' because one of the things we're really committed to is giving all women an opportunity to play in a supportive atmosphere. We have women who have played varsity college softball and women who've never played softball at all. Most teams [in this league] have the philosophy that everybody gets to play regardless of ability so there isn't a sense that your best ten players are on the field and your subs sit on the bench. Everybody plays an equal amount.

"There's a rule in the league, too, that you don't ride the other team. You cheer for your own team, you cheer for good plays, and it's really a faux pas to say something from the bench about the other team. And one of my favorite rules is if the team that's at bat thinks that the other pitcher is too fast, you can tell her to slow down. And that's sort of an arbitrary decision. Everybody sort of has a sense of what's an O.K. speed and what's not an O.K. speed. And it's pretty much accepted among all the teams.

"We play fast pitch rules, basically, so we get to steal, but we play with ten players so you have four outfielders. And you can also have a pinch runner from the plate so that women who pull their hamstrings in the first part of the season, or their quadriceps, can still take their at bats but somebody runs for them.

"Occasionally, we've had a whole team of people [who are highly competitive]. They either have to change the way they play or they sort of get identified as the league 'bad guys.' They win all their games, and nobody likes them. Generally, when that's happened, they don't stick around the league long or they change their attitude; they start to loosen up a little bit. That's gone on with a couple of teams.

"Another rule I should tell you about is if you're fifteen runs behind, you have the option of saying, "That's it. We give up.' There's also an unspoken rule that if your team is *way* ahead, you stop stealing bases and stuff like that—you sort of let up a little bit. The other thing that's happened sometimes is when you're totally unmatched—like a new team in the league and a team that's been around awhile—what we've done is we've stopped the game and said, 'Do you want to just split up the players, and half of us will play with you and half of you will come with us?' And we'll continue the game that way, just so we can play instead of [just] clobbering someone. But it's always up to the team that's losing to make the decision to do that.

"[On the other hand], when we go out on the field, we want to win, and we play as hard as we can. And we don't like to lose. And there are some very competitive women in the league, like me, but it's relearning a competitive ethic. That's what it's like for me. It's like, 'Yeah, I want to win, but there are certain things I'm not willing to do to win.' Like it's not O.K. with me to make another team feel terrible or to make fun of another team, or rub their noses in it. Yes, I'm going to celebrate, and I'm going to try my hardest; and I'm *never* going to do anything less than my best; and I certainly *love* making the tough plays at third base or hitting a home run; but it's a respectful competition, and we try to keep that in mind.

"And we're not always successful either. There are times when ugly stuff gets said and done on the field, but when it happens we try to work it out instead of just letting it go. I don't want to leave you with the impression that people are not trying to win, because we definitely are. That's part of the fun of it—to go for it—but not at any cost. The best game is when everybody plays really hard and feels really good about each other."

Jo and Astrid, The Wilder Ones
Minneapolis, Minnesota

"We try to emphasize the positive. When a player makes an error, nobody knows more intensely than she that she messed up. . . . What we try to do is build each other up so that the next time that woman is handling the ball her confidence will have resumed and she'll be able to handle it and not still be punishing herself from her last error." (Jo)

"I started out playing very individualistically and concentrating mainly on how I was doing, how I was improving. And more and more I feel now that I'm striving to work with other members of the team as a unit. I think, ironically, this has come about through our newly set goal which is to become more serious and more competitive about our play. I think what this is going to do is to force us to cooperate more and act collectively." (Astrid)[6]

Kathy Phillips, The Wildcat Strikes
San Francisco, California

"The team I presently play on—The Wildcat Strikes— formerly had a coach who emphasized competition and played those she thought were skilled while benching or 'sticking in right field' poorer players. We decided this season to meet and discuss how we wanted to run our team. At the meeting we arrived at a philosophy that, while we assumed everyone would do their best to win, we would not bench someone or put them in a position they really didn't want to play solely for the sake of winning. Every player on the team would play equal time whenever possible, and each person would have a primary and a back-up position based on combination of her desires, her skills, and team need. Right field (a position viewed as unsatisfying) would be rotated. We also decided to rotate our coaching, with team members taking turns but with decision-making about what to work on, the line-up, etc., made by shared decision by the whole team. We agreed to try very hard to communicate any problems with the whole team as soon as they arose. Some people wanted a coached team focused on winning and split off to form their own team. The rest of us remained and stuck more or less to the above agreement. Some of us found out we hated being the coach and we had our struggles, but we did come in first place and were very proud of ourselves."

Kate Clinton: "I love this season because it's spring and that means we are in softball. I love softball. I play third base. (Do you want to see my shins?) I'm on this great team—you would love my team. Last year they made Michael Jackson our team mascot because he wears a glove on one hand for no apparent reason. I love my team—they're an interesting mix of women. We've worked hard with a lot of these women and they keep their eyes open now when they catch the ball and it's really beautiful. Women who are, like, not into competition—now tell me, aren't those usually the women who come with the brand new two-inch cleats—on the first day? On my team, there are also some women who just can't get into the coach-player dynamic. They cannot deal with the hierarchy of that. So we do a lot of processing on our team. Velveeta should be our team sponsor."

Winning Is Everything (Well, Sort Of) — Four Stories

Stephie, Sidetrack, Chicago, Illinois

"There are teams you can either play on to have fun or to play to win. I like to play to win because I have fun at it. I'm very competitive that way. I don't like to play on a softball team just to play because to me that's a waste of my time. I could just do that on any Sunday—at a picnic or something. That's always tough with some teams, as far as the coaches go: who do you pick to play? Do you play to win or do you play to have fun? Because if you play to have fun, you pick everybody—everybody gets to play. [Otherwise] feelings get hurt."

Beth, The Hags, Los Angeles, California

"My team of long-standing—The Hags—plays as well as possible—sometimes quite well, and we have games that seem like one long magic moment—but we never do better than second. I think the biggest problem most women have is knowing what wanting to win is about. That disturbs me. It is hard to reconcile playing truly competitive ball with playing because we are friends and love to play together, and I guess our compromise has limited our trophy-taking. . . . I took out a second baseman with no forethought and no guilt for the first time ever the other night, so I suppose that is a sign of some growth."

Paula Sanchez, Synergy, Chicago, Illinois

"Everybody [on the team knows] that they were picked [specially to play on this team], even though we all knew a lot more people. And they felt that that was kind of special, that for some reason they were picked to play with this group of people. So they all came to each game feeling special. And out of that came our main goal: to win the gay league and then go on and hopefully make a good showing at the [Gay] World Series. So our softball goal was to win that league. We played in another league and were going to use that for practice and we almost won that league too."

Foul Ball: A True Story

A woman from Philadelphia recalled how, playing outfield, she ran to catch a high fly ball one day. As she was running, the ground suddenly gave way under her feet, and she found herself chest deep—in a septic tank. Her teammates rushed anxiously to where she had disappeared into the ground and peered over the edge, concern etched on their faces. And almost in unison they asked, "Did you catch the ball?"

Perception/Deception

The outward appearance of the game is affected by something even more fundamental than philosophies of play: how we see ourselves as lesbian athletes. This perception is shaped by our internalized homophobia, the amount of support we have gotten for being athletic, and how we think others see us. The overlap and intermingling of these factors, through the filter of our personalities, creates a unique relationship between each player and the game—a relationship that is never static and decidedly complex.

How We See Ourselves

Gyacko: "I enjoy the literary/political women because most of the time they make up for the lack of womanhood found in most jocks. It is sexy to find a woman who is gay and who enjoys being a woman, instead of a hard-core bulldyke who gives lesbians a bad name and bad appearance."

Miller Lite Report on Women in Sports: A statement that participants disagreed with strongly was: "Participation in sports diminishes a woman's femininity."[7]

Achy Obejas: "In Chicago, I've attended a few games, as a spectator, and have been pretty put off. It seems pretty macho out there sometimes. . . ."

Janice Kaplan: "Shirley [Babashoff] was worried about her image. Since swimmers generally keep their hair short to be practical, Shirley grew hers very long and made fun of the other women's 'butch' look. At the Olympics, she targeted her snipes at the broad-shouldered East Germans, hinting they had become the best in the world by being more man than woman."[8]

A sister teammate of mine in Chicago: "Hey! I have to keep my fingernails long—I don't want to be totally unfeminine."

Describe *myself* as an athletic woman? The adjectives and phrases I would use all have—or I would ascribe to them—positive meanings: healthy, fit, vital, muscular, aware of and comfortable with my body, constantly striving for improvement, cooperative, supportive, enthusiastic, and reasonably attractive. While many straight women athletes take up a defensive posture (not only going out of their way to appear feminine themselves, but also ridiculing others in contrast), and while many lesbians themselves see jocks as masculine-looking (as the quotes above illustrate), most of us have generally positive self-images.

For some, that positive self-image is only possible by embracing certain aspects of femininity: long fingernails, clean-shaven legs, a svelte figure, or stylish haircut. Looking feminine, of course, is most often a thinly veiled concern about sexual preference, as *feminine* is frequently a euphemism for *heterosexual* woman and *unfeminine*— or *butch* or *masculine* or sometimes even *muscular*—are all often euphemisms for *lesbian*. Nowhere are the effects of these correlations more visible than in college and university athletic departments, where researcher Sharon Guthrie "was able to conclude convincingly that the level of homophobia she found . . . makes women fearful of losing their jobs. And it causes female athletes to adopt 'apologetic' behavior, such as overemphasizing the external trappings of femininity."[9] Women in team sports are also subject to high levels of homophobia, both from others and from what they've internalized and are, therefore, prime candidates for adopting apologetic behavior.

Nevertheless, there is a healthy proportion of the softball-dyke population that has managed not to be constrained by such fears. For these women, it seems that looking feminine is outside of their consciousness and not something they concern themselves with much. For some, this is so because they simply take it for granted that as women they are feminine by definition: "pertaining to a woman or girl . . . belonging to the female sex."[10] For others, it is a refusal to characterize themselves using other people's standards.

How Others See Us
(And How We Think They See Us)

R. J.: "Society here views athletic women as acting and looking too masculine—they don't like it and don't want to put up with it."

Suzi: "Straight society has taken quite a turn [for the better] as far as women in athletics. However, many still feel that feminine is nonathletic and preferable. My experiences growing up athletic sadden me as I gave up, for a period in high school, some things I loved because [they] didn't fit in . . . ."

Harry Edwards: "In America a female's athletic competence is seen to detract from her womanliness ('She can throw a ball, bat and run like a boy'). For this reason, many females never become involved in the most popular sports." And, "most women are forced by cultural definitions to choose between being an athlete (thereby facing the barely hidden suspicions as to their heterosexuality) and being a woman."[11]

Polly: "Society looks on women athletes in physical sports as lesbians, but I think that view may be starting to change."

Patricia McLaughlin: "In the old days, women who played on coed teams often wore their baggiest, oldest sweats as an earnest reminder that they cared more about the game than the outfit. But now that so many girls start playing softball in school and keep it up, 'fashion is sneaking in,' according to Kathy Button of Wilson Sporting Goods. . . . It's a sign of the times that . . . girls don't see any conflict between looking good and being able to nail a runner at the plate."[12]

J. F. Garman's master's thesis study found that gymnasts were viewed as the most feminine female athletes and that softball players were identified as the least feminine.[13]

Janice Kaplan: "The CBS officials who had hired [Debbie Meyer] to do occasional commentary on the 'Sports Spectacular' show eased her out, feeling that she was too heavy to appear on camera. They couldn't promote her as either jock or woman—she was an indeterminate blob."[14]

Susan Begg: "I think many people consider women who play [softball] seriously to be butch although there always seem to be a lot of straight men and women fans that support the teams that play well regardless. . . . Staying fit is more desirable to society in general now, so there is less of the tomboy stigma in being a player than [there was] ten years ago."

Mary Boutilier and Lucinda SanGiovanni: "The media focus on women athletes for nonathletic reasons. . . . Women gain attention for being good-looking, feminine, well-dressed, ladylike, petite, and controversial, rather than for their athletic achievements."[15]

There are few who would argue with the statement that athletic women are more accepted now than they were in the past. But this acceptance comes, generally, only with qualifications—the primary one being that athletic women adhere to societally prescribed standards of femininity.

The issue of femininity is one that arises again and again in discussions of women and sports. Generally, the debate has centered around the question of whether athletic women are—or can be—feminine. And for most of us, no matter which side of the debate we're on, it never occurs to us that *the question may be wrong.* Dr. Ruth Bennett, a psychologist, puts it well in an exchange with Betty Hicks: "The myth purveyors say women in sports are masculine, muscular, aggressive, dominant, lesbian, success-oriented. 'What if they are?' retorts Bennett. 'Why should so many pages be devoted to defending, excusing, begging, or apologizing for the desire of girls and women to pursue all forms of movement activity?'"[16] So what? *That's* the question we should be asking. So what if we *aren't* "feminine"? So what if we are muscular, aggressive, and lesbian? Why should those terms, when applied to women, automatically be construed as negative? As Boutilier and SanGiovanni point out, "To ask if women can remain women and still play sports means that . . .one accepts the white, male, heterosexual, middle-class definitions of women and sport."[17]

When we accept others' definitions of us as our own definitions, we risk limiting ourselves. If we accept that being feminine—in the conventional sense of being weak, gentle, passive, and glamorous—is important, we may not permit ourselves to engage fully with softball—whether that means not sliding because we'll get dirty; wearing certain types of jewelry that could put us in danger of injury; insisting we're unable to throw the ball hard and accurately; being more concerned—or even just as concerned—with how we look than with how we're playing. It is not that we should go out of our way to be masculine and macho but, rather, that we should be more concerned with who we are than who we "ought" to be. It is also not that we should necessarily devote our whole lives to softball:

we should be able to put ourselves into softball as much as we want to and not let ourselves be intimidated into holding back. Fortunately, from what I've seen and heard, holding back is not exactly a problem for softball dykes. As Alix Dobkin says, "As with everything else they do, lesbians are 100 percent invested in softball."

Notes

1. Betty Hicks, "Lesbian Athletes," *Christopher Street* 4, no. 3 (October/November 1979): 49. (Abner Doubleday is the man often credited with inventing baseball.)

2. Toni McNaron, "An Interview with the Wilder Ones," *So's Your Old Lady*, no. 10 (September 1975), p. 7.

3. R. R. Knudson, *Zanboomer* (New York: Dell Publishing, 1978), p. 1.

4. *Miller Lite Report on Women in Sports* (New York: Women's Sports Foundation, 1985), p.11.

5. Mary A. Boutilier and Lucinda SanGiovanni, *The Sporting Woman* (Champaign, Ill.: Human Kinetics Publishers, 1983), p. 121.

6. McNaron, pp. 7, 8.

7. *Miller Lite Report on Women in Sports*, p. 11.

8. Janice Kaplan, *Women and Sports* (New York: Viking Press, 1979), p. 67.

9. Michele Kort, "High Marks for Homophobia," *Women's Sports* (November 1982), p. 20.

10. *Random House Dictionary of the English Language*, unabridged ed. (New York: Random House, Inc., 1973), s.v. "feminine."

11. Harry Edwards, "Desegregating Sexist Sport," in *Out of the Bleachers: Writings on Women and Sport*, ed. Stephanie L. Twin (Old Westbury, N.Y.: Feminist Press, 1979), pp. 190-91.

12. Patricia McLaughlin, "Diamond Duds: There's No Uniform Opinion on Why Softball Wears Well," *Chicago Tribune*, May 15, 1988.

13. J. F. Garman, "A Study of Attitudes toward Athletic Competition for Women" (Master's thesis, University of California, Santa Barbara, 1969), quoted in Ellen W. Gerber et al., *The American Woman in Sport* (Reading, Mass.: Addison-Wesley, 1974), p. 363.

14. Kaplan, p. 63.

15. Boutilier and SanGiovanni, pp. 44-45.

16. Hicks, p. 50.

17. Boutilier and SanGiovanni, p. 117.

Chapter 7

Who's At Bat, Jocks Or Feminists? Or, Will The Real Lesbian Community Please Stand Up

One of the first things a typical lesbian learns is that there is no such thing as a typical lesbian. As many lesbians as there are, there are nearly as many different kinds: different interests, races, politics, activities, priorities, cultures, ages, and classes. These differences manifest themselves in who we hang out with, where we congregate, what we join (or don't), and how we choose to identify ourselves. Consequently, big cities supporting large lesbian communities—that is, communities that can provide lesbians with a variety of options—generally have fairly distinct subcommunities: bar dykes, jocks, politically active dykes, culturally involved dykes, and the home entertainment/potluck crowd, to mention just a few. Though the subcommunities are sometimes further subdivided—for instance, the jocks often group themselves by sport—each subcommunity is essentially cohesive, socializing together both within and outside of the context of their chosen activities.

But as distinct as the subcommunities can be, there is usually some overlap—in many communities, to cite one example, a lot of bar dykes are also jocks. And in small towns, there are virtually *no* divisions between parts of the community: they can't afford them. As Ellen Heimbuck of South Dakota reports, "[In] the. . . places I've lived there was no split. We didn't have much support, so we had to stick together. Everyone learned to appreciate each other and support each other. It made us stronger."

In major metropolitan areas, however, sheer numbers, along with the multiplicity of options available, often result in subcommunities that have little or no contact with one another. And nowhere is the split between parts of the community more noticeable than between the jocks and the feminists. While it is not always true that jocks are jocks and feminists are feminists and never the twain shall meet—Albuquerque and Washington, D.C., to name but two places, are reputed to have whole teams and leagues that describe themselves as feminist—jocks often don't identify as feminists, and politically active feminists are seldom jocks. Like any groups of people that have little

"... And now I'd like to introduce the woman who organized the lesbian world into two softball teams..."

contact with one another, they often harbor misconceptions about each other, and there are misunderstandings between the two groups.

Linda J. Adams: "As both an active athlete and lover of women's music events, I sometimes feel like I have a foot in two completely different worlds. I'm surrounded by lesbians in both of these settings, but . . . there's very little overlap."[1]

Choosing Up Sides: Where Does The Split Come From?

In communities where there are easily identifiable groups of jocks and literary/political women (most or all of whom would consider themselves feminists), the division into two distinct subcommunities is often simply pragmatic. Such a division pares the community into more manageable pieces. In lesbian communities that are very large, one can have a sense of not knowing anyone and, consequently, feeling overwhelmed, alienated, or lonely. The subcommunities both reduce the number of people one is confronted with and give one a starting base for relating, a common ground of similar interests. It is only natural that women with similar interests should gravitate toward one another, and so such groupings evolve naturally.

What this theory of "natural evolution" doesn't explain, however, is how or why women in sports and nonathletic lesbian feminists form, as Linn ni Cobhan observes, "two separate camps, each somewhat hostile, suspicious, and often ignorant of the other."[2] The concept of *enemy camps* is not consistent from community to community, of course, or even from individual to individual in a given community. But these qualities (hostility, suspicion, and ignorance) are present often enough—particularly the ignorance —to warrant further investigation. There are a number of possible explanations.

Class

Barbara Grier: "Earlier [in the forties and fifties] you had a greater cross-section of women [playing ball] than you have now because now there is a more stratified community. In our incredible dash to socialize, and 'socialism-ize' our community, i.e., to cut out class boundaries, we have actually created more rigid class boundaries. Because in the early days you either hung out in bars, you lived all by yourself in isolation (or, as the old *Ladder* saying went, 'Living alone in egoism a deux'), or you belonged to the ball teams. And the ball team groups probably had a wider social strata than it does now. That is to say, it had lower-class women, lower-middle-class women, middle-class women, and even an occasional upper-middle-class woman who, because of her love of athletics, would deign to run around with that crew. Now, of course, it has become very much a lower-middle-class milieu for the most part; there are some middle-class women, but now I think it's much more isolated because there are whole other communities for the women to take part in."

This view is not uncommon. And though in some communities there may actually be a division between jocks and feminists along class lines, my own experience in Chicago and the experiences of women from a wide range of cities and towns across the country reveal that softball dykes come from backgrounds that span the different classes. Moreover, many of those who originally came from blue-collar families are now themselves white-collar workers and professionals.

If it seems unlikely that class differences form the dividing line between the two groups, then where does this notion of stratification come from? Basically, softball as a whole is commonly perceived as a lower-class activity or as "the sport of the masses." This perception is not completely out of line in that more people play softball in this country than any other team sport.[3] Furthermore, baseball/softball doesn't require much in the way of equipment or facilities—or, therefore, money—and is accessible, accordingly, even to the near-poor. As one woman from the All-American Girls Professional Baseball League put it, "In those days [the 1940s], all girls had was baseball—and tennis and golf, if you had money. And we didn't have any money."[4] Softball/baseball is one of the few sports that is accessible in this way. Yet to assume, therefore, that *only* people from lower-class backgrounds play is decidedly an error, as any survey of softball dykes reveals.

Then, too, jocks are made up of more than just softball dykes. But any of the rough-and-tumble sports (soccer, rugby, basketball, football) are viewed as lower-class activities—*especially* when played by women. In any case, because softball dykes make up the largest—or, at any rate, the most noticeable—percentage of lesbian jocks, and because they are frequently involved in other sports as well, their interactions with feminists in the community are undoubtedly representative of lesbian jocks in general.

"Stereotypes Are The Problem, As Usual"

Or so says a woman from L.A., assessing why she thinks a split in the community exists there. And indeed, stereotypes—on both sides—are a major factor. They are evident in discussions of class backgrounds and political-awareness levels or in speculation on any other differences (perceived or real) between the two groups.

When the split exists, it is not surprising that each group develops stereotypic images of the other, given they have little interaction. What we find ourselves with then is the chicken-and-egg question: which came first, the stereotypes or the split? Trying to answer that would be a long, tedious, and almost certainly futile task. In any case, stereotypes help to maintain any division that exists, and any division helps promote stereotypes—a symbiotic relationship that is not particularly healthy.

Level Of Political Consciousness

Mary Boutilier and Lucinda SanGiovanni: "There is a noticeable absence of a feminist perspective among sporting women as well as an overwhelming silence among most feminists regarding sports."[5]

Along with stereotypes, each groups's relationship to lesbian/feminist politics contributes to the division between them. Feminists often see jocks as nonfeminist (or even antifeminist) in their approach to a wide range of issues, including race and class. Jocks are also seen as not pulling their own weight in the battle for women's and gay rights. On the other hand, feminists are often perceived by jocks as being uptight, politically pushy, and unconcerned about and/or unaware of the issues confronting athletic women. As for their own relationship to politics, jocks frequently find that their interests just lie elsewhere. As She-Her says, "I don't have the time or motivation to participate. Other things are more important to me." Though neither side's view of the other is completely false, there is a lack of understanding by both of the separate realities that motivate each.

Side 1: The Jocks
Sizing Up The Opponent

Stephie: "What do you mean by feminist? When I think of feminists, I think of hairy armpits, hairy legs, ERA all the way. . . . I believe in equal pay, yes. [But] if I was straight and went out on a date with a guy, I'd still want the guy to open the door for me. I don't think I'm a feminist. I believe in equal rights—don't get me wrong—and I believe in equal pay, but. . . . I know some women who are feminists but I'm not like that."

R. J.: "Most of the women who play softball in this community do not associate with the literary/political women. But I do associate with these women on a friendly basis. One woman lawyer in town is very interested in my views—we talk a lot—and the more I get to know her, the more I feel there will always be a split in communities like this one in that aspect."

Mei: "I've had some incidents with [politically active] people who've told me, 'I hate jocks.' "

Mary Farmer: "There are a lot of 'feminists' who have no sense of other parts of lesbian culture. That's my opinion. I've seen it happen, and it's very narrow-minded, and I don't appreciate it myself. It's like cutting off a piece of our lesbian identity."

Mo: "I'm a fun-loving person, like to let my hair down and have a good time, talk about a lot of *different* subjects, and am not always *so serious*. My impression is [that] the literary/political women are too serious, seem to be more separatist, and don't know how 'to let their hair down' and act *silly!*"

Barbara Grier: "Years and years ago I was invited to speak at a now-defunct coffeehouse in San Francisco, on a West Coast tour. And I went and spoke, and there were two women who were glaring at me in the crowd of thirty-five or forty in the little coffeehouse. . . . When I went into the john [later] they were in the other stall, and one was saying to the other, 'Can you imagine that! She said we're not oppressed.' In other words, if they didn't have that oppression to hug to their bosom, what the hell else did they have in life? Their reality was being a member of an oppressed group. And my attitude toward that is, 'Bullshit. You're only oppressed if you let somebody push you.' And that's just a difference in attitude. But the political people are pissed at the jocks [because] the jocks say, 'Life's short, the girls are pretty. The beer is good. Don't give me any of this political crap.' "

Feminists tend to get a bad rap all around. Society defines them as man-hating, aggressive in a pushy political way, lesbian, and humorless. Jocks, in addition, tend to view feminists as elitist snobs who don't know how to lighten up and have a good time. Jocks also feel that feminists don't have any sense of the female athlete's concerns and problems. There may be elements of truth here and there among these allegations, but so much generalization has occurred that feminists are largely misunderstood.

Separatism and hatred of men, for example, is far from the rule among feminists. Feminists *do* hold men account-able for their actions, refusing to automatically accept traditionally defined roles as legitimate excuses for incon-siderate, chauvinistic, or elitist behaviors on the part of men; and they refuse to be submissive in the face of obvious imbalances of power. Consequently, they are seen as hating men when what they actually dislike are certain *behaviors* of men.

Similarly, though feminists are fervent in their pursuit for equality of all kinds, it is because they have learned that change will not come about unless those who are oppressed *make* it come about—those in power are not likely to turn any of that power over willingly to someone else. The problem is that not everyone sees or feels oppression in the same way. Much of the difference between how women respond politically to oppression has to do with levels of energy and acceptance. Feminists are more willing to give up personal, immediate pleasures to work for a greater good in some future. Self-defined nonfeminists are less likely to be aware of oppression or more willing to accept a certain amount of inconvenience as "life." Furthermore, jocks (and other nonfeminists) often perceive political activism as risky in terms of protecting their lesbian identity from exposure. Or, they see it as time away from other, more immediate concerns: "Life's short, the girls are pretty. The beer's good," as Barbara Grier has pointed out. In other words, different people weigh costs and benefits differently: not everyone has the same priorities, interests, and aptitudes.

Then there is the issue of feminist frivolity—or, reputedly, the lack thereof. In reference to the long-standing charge that feminists have no sense of humor, feminist humorist Kate Clinton reminds us, "Men have used humor against women for so long that we do not trust humor —we know implicitly whose butt is the butt of their jokes."[6] But now, with the cultivation of feminist humor, funny feminists are making themselves known in greater numbers. According to Clinton, feminist humor is "based more on the egalitarian notion of stand-with comedy and does not rely on the put-down of fun-poking."[7] Feminists have a keen sense of irony. What they *don't* find funny are put-downs.

The second issue concerning feminists and fun has to do with their supposed inability to have any—with not knowing how to "let their hair down and act silly." In fact, it's simply a matter of personal taste: what is enjoyable to one person or group of people is not necessarily enjoyable to another.

As for feminists being more uptight, there may be some truth to this. Feminists—by and large nonathletes, or at least nonparticipants in team sports—may feel less at home in their bodies and more at home with their minds. As a consequence, their fun naturally revolves more around lively conversation and witty word play than around physical activity, physical humor, and sexual innuendo—some of the things the jock circles I've been involved in seem to deal with comfortably.

What seems most true of feminists is that they don't, in general, have much knowledge of or appreciation for the special problems confronting female athletes. There has been passing attention paid to equality of opportunity for women in sports as part of a push for equality for women in all walks of life, but sports have not been the focus of much critical or philosophical attention from feminists. Despite the self-esteem, self-confidence, and experience with teamwork and cooperation that participation in athletics affords, feminists have not embraced athletic opportunity for women with the same zeal that they have embraced opportunities in other areas of women's lives. And women whose livelihood is not tied in some way to athletics—as is that of professional and amateur athletes and physical educators—don't really understand the implicit and explicit constraints athletic women face.

Jocks Sizing Up Jocks

Pat Griffin: "Homophobia, in the established athletic community, whether it be college varsity athletics or whatever, is so paralyzing that I think that feminist women—feminist lesbians in particular—who are not part of that real serious athletic world tend to see apolitical women jocks as sort of like queen bees. I think that women who are in the athletic world—particularly if they're associated with college athletics—are under male control. And it's a very homophobic world, and their jobs are on the line or their spots on the team if they're athletes. And that's serious. And the homophobia is just unbelievable. Some of the horror stories about things that happen to athletic women make it hard for them to take on the label *feminist*, which is, in terms of labels, a scary label in addition to *athlete*— and forget *lesbian*. Because feminist and lesbian are practically synonymous to a lot of the men, particularly."

Martina Navratilova: "I've lost so many endorsements because of that. It's sad. It gets to the highest level, and then it's, 'Oh, isn't she gay? Or, hasn't she had relationships with women? Or, isn't she living with a woman?' The president of a corporation may be my best friend, but he still won't take that chance because of the public. He might get five bad letters and a hundred good ones, but the five bad ones are the ones that matter. I know also why sometimes I get boos on the tennis court from some people. They're booing my lifestyle, rather than me as a human being."[8]

Missy Myers: "My sense is that there is something of a split [between the two parts of the community] in that most jocks are not heavily into literary/political issues (and vice versa), but that it is not antagonistic in any sense."

Lynn Rossellini: "An openly gay player would be cut off from product endorsements and teaching jobs. . . . [And if an accomplished lesbian athlete *were* to come out,] instead of being a leader of women in sports, she'd be the lesbian athlete."[9]

Polly: "A lot of intellectual women think jocks don't care about 'culture.' "

Laurie: "I tend not to push [political] things on or at people. Granted sometimes we have to, but I guess I am a bit apathetic to those issues."

Jean Claiborne: "Personally, myself, I'm not much into any other community activities. We don't have a real strong lesbian community in Nashville as far as I know. I guess they have a place where they meet and a news-letter or something. They have dances every now and then. . . . And I've gone occasionally because some of my friends have said they're having a dance, but I'm not into. . .the Women's Movement and such."

Florence: "I think the problem is that too many of the jocks are just there to play and I guess that's O.K. if that's your purpose, but I think there's a need for them to go beyond that and give a little bit more—including myself—and contribute to the community and unite it and make it a stronger place to live in. And I think that's probably the biggest dividing line—that jocks go out there and play, party, and go home and that's it. And the only thing that they associate with the gay lifestyle is maybe the softball. The political people will have [an awareness of the gay lifestyle] more in a higher level, all-around social level. . . . I'm more involved in playing sports than political issues. I'm not involved politically at all. I mean I go and I support it and I contribute [monetarily]. And when there's an issue I like to be there at some of the rallies. But to be honest with you, I'm not dedicated in the political world. And that's something, in part, that I need to grow into. What pulls me more into the gay community is the sports because, regardless of if I were [in the community] or not, I would love sports. And being that the gay women that I find are mostly involved in sports, I find myself [having] more of a jock attitude. So I am there to play sports. . . . That's not enough. And that's probably a weakness—that all the jocks have to realize that it's good to play, and it's nice to identify yourself when you're playing, but that's only temporar[y], and you have to go beyond that. We all have to learn to move on. And that's the biggest downfall of jocks. And I'm part of it."

Mary Boutilier and Lucinda SanGiovanni: "Of all the stigmas noted, that of sexual preference has a special significance for sporting women. The issue of lesbianism remains a dormant but ever-present and undis-. cussed topic. . . . The myth of masculinization of athletic women has always been a societal concern. Mere participation in sport can cast a woman's sexual preference into question, just as participation in ballet can for men. What makes this issue particularly problematic is that the lesbian athlete is rarely a feminist. Thus, she is taught and encouraged to accept the social definition of her preference as deviant. She seeks merely to hide it, to keep it private, and to avoid the sanctions that would be forthcoming if her sexual orientation were uncovered."[10]

Rita Mae Brown: "Keep in mind that women in physical education are terrified of public lesbianism because of the manner in which their profession has been downgraded by our society."[11]

Miller Lite Report on Women in Sports: "If feminism is defined as being committed to equality for women in all aspects of life, how strong would you say your feminist views are? Very strong, 41%; strong, 25%; somewhat strong, 20%; not very strong, 6%; I do not consider myself a feminist, 8%."[12]

Jocks are often, by their own admission, not very interested in the cultural aspects of our community and not terribly invested in politics (lesbian, feminist, or otherwise). But part of this low-profile community stance has to do with self-preservation. The small percentage of softball dykes who are P.E. teachers, or otherwise make their living with athletics, bear the heaviest burden. But any women who play sports—especially sports in which you *really* sweat, get dirty, and fraternize a lot, as in team sports—are immediately suspect in the eyes of the world. Despite the amazing progress in public attitudes about athletic women, women who are perceived as too invested in sports are subject to speculation not only about their sexual preference but about their very identity as women as well. They are seen as not feminine enough. Because of this, and in order to combat these suspicions, many athletic women dissociate themselves as much as possible from any other activities or doctrines that would further incriminate them. As Pat Griffin says, "feminist and lesbian are practically synonymous" for many people.

"Another reason for a woman athlete's seeming disregard for feminist issues may well be that, by participating in athletic competition, she feels she has already done

her part for women's rights," says Linn ni Cobhan.[13] Jocks
are struggling for equality in the arena they know best and
where, therefore, they can make their greatest contribution; because of their love of sports, they can really put
their heart and soul into the struggle. Jocks and feminists
are both fighting for equality of opportunity for women—
just on different fronts.

Side 2: The Feminists
(And How They See Jocks)

Rita Mae Brown: "A self-appointed contingent of physical education majors burst into my room . . . . Frightened past reason, these wild-eyed women informed me
that if I even hinted that they were Lesbians or that
any of their beloved faculty fell into that damned category, they would kill me."[14]

Rhonda Craven: "I think there's some snobbery involved. I think that a lot of the more political women
tend to see the jocks as anti-intellectuals or something.
And I think that might be a carryover from what people perceive is the situation among men. In some cases
it is true. A lot of people who are into 'jockdom' have
absolutely no interest in things political, literary, or
otherwise. I think there's also the perception that these
women who are jocks are much more into partying,
into drinking, into being rowdy. As a result, because
those are things you're not supposed to do if you're
wanting to be PC, there isn't a lot of mingling. Because
the folks who are more intellectual or political might
be more into having quiet gatherings where they sit
around and talk about the latest book that came out
by someone or the new newspaper or anything like

that, while a lot of the jocks sit around and talk about jock stuff—you know, the next game and what happened the last game or something like that. So there seems to be very little mixing because there's this perception, often quite accurate, that they have absolutely nothing in common. The jocks tend, a lot of times, to hang out in bars more than political lesbians. The bar where all the political dykes hung out [in Chicago] closed because they weren't getting much business, because the political women didn't drink that much. The jocks tended to go to other bars, it seemed. . . . I don't see [the split] as animosity. I think it's just that they don't see the common ground that would make them mingle. I think it's there, but neither is particularly interested in seeking it out unless some of the individuals have been friends someplace else. Then there's usually some joking around about, you know, 'Oh, you're such a jock,' 'All you do is keep your head in a book,' etc. But other than that, I think there's peaceful coexistence."

Liz: "The jocks have more fun."

Mary Boutilier and Lucinda SanGiovanni feel that the heightened homophobia that exists in women's athletics is, in part, because few women in sport are feminist in an ideological sense and "leave to feminists ('Yes, I play sports but I'm not a feminist') the more difficult task of articulating the existence of lesbianism in sport."[15]

Pat Parker: "There are a lot more jocks [than feminists]. And political consciousness is not very high [with them]. I've actually had to sit my team down and lecture to them about what kind of chatter is permitted on our team. . . . I won't tolerate [any put-downs] from anyone on my team toward any player that's playing with them or on the other team . . . . And that's *not* the norm . . . . And I think the thing is that many of the women who are feminists move away from competitive sports as being not feminist. I'm not one to argue either side."

Achy Obejas: "I think it might be . . . appropriate to ask the jocks why they're so hostile sometimes to the nonathletic, more intellectual women."

Toni Armstrong, Jr.: I have seen a difference between the two communities [jocks and feminists]. Those in the political community tend to be more political, cultural, active. They seem to have a broader-based community consciousness and more of an interest in what's going on in the world. And all of them are pretty different in the politics that they believe [in], but there's some sort of idea that we're all part of a bigger picture. Whereas— although I hate to generalize—the jocks that I've known over the years seem to focus totally on their individual lives; they're going to make their lives good, no matter what, and don't focus on the bigger picture. And that generally means not being very open as lesbians, even to other lesbians—not seeing or valuing much by way of community, not really caring much about the bigger picture or the politics. They want their job, their lover, their home, their safety. . . . The women that I've known, that I've ended up being friends with who are jocks, have been medium-receptive to women's culture stuff. They ended up liking going to concerts and even festivals, and I've noted a real shift in their consciousness level. But it's like they're starting at ground zero. It doesn't seem like there's a real *resistance* there, but it seems they don't get any lesbian-specific consciousness raising from the community they're in, even when they're with all lesbians on their team.

The jocks that I've known have been predominantly white suburban women, and it could make a real difference if we're *not* talking about white women. They tend to have gotten the benefit of education around racism and classism, and other issues that feminism addresses. They're not feminist, first of all—they think "women's libbers," and they make jokes about it. It's really low consciousness. I think when the political women collide with the jock women, the political women demand accountability. And the jocks are not at all used to that. They're not even used to being *open*, let alone somebody challenging them on all these oppressive behaviors and attitudes they, as part of the larger society, just accept.

Teaming Up: When Jocks Are Feminists

Melinda Shaw: "There are some women who participate in athletics who are involved very seriously in cultural and political events. This closes the gap between these two groups. Many of our fans are nonjocks who respect those who do play, as the jocks respect the roles of the other women."

Bea: "In our case, the team I have played on since 1979 is sponsored by the women's bookstore in the city, which is feminist-run. So, we are fortunate to have structured ways of joining the arts, sports, and women's politics. A number of locally active NOW women are also on the team—so we have a number of sets touching each other."

Celeste Methot: "From what I know of both Nashville and Atlanta, [the community] is pretty homogeneous,

[though] I know in Atlanta there was somewhat of a dis-
tinction between those people who were very politically
active and real big in the community and the rest of
us who were just active on a mediocre level and who
were jocks. There were people who had absolutely nothing to do with sports; they're just into their politics.
There was a team in Atlanta called the Amazons, and
that was a real political team. They had somewhat of
a following of the feminist crowd. . . . But when we
were all in social settings we mixed just fine."

P. L.: "[About a year ago], I would definitely have said
there was a stronger split, but now I don't think it's
that strong [because] I've gotten to know [political] people. . . . That's changed things a lot. . . . I've gotten
to know [some feminists] more as individuals. [And]
I've had many arguments with people—[we] argue all
the time about politics and stuff like that. . . . It's not
like we can't discuss our opinions about things—actually,
I've been enlightened about a lot of stuff."

Not every community is split this way along jock/fem-
inist lines. Women in Berkeley, San Diego, and Houston,
in addition to the previously mentioned Albuquerque and
Washington, D.C., felt confident that no such split existed there and were surprised to hear that such disunities
occur anywhere. Still, Chicago, among numerous other
areas of the country, has clearly had a history of distinct
borders between jocks and feminists. Although that seems
to be changing at a painfully slow rate, it *does* seem to
be changing.
    My own experience with this may not be entirely typi-
cal, as Chicago has long had the reputation of being the
most segregated city in the country. And though that
epithet has generally been used to describe the race situ-

ation, it seems to spill over into other areas as well, including gay male and lesbian relations, and *within* the lesbian community. The result of this is that there is very little intermingling between the different subsets.

By way of illustration, in the lesbian community, where I have been active in our cultural life since I first arrived, none of my literary friends even seemed to know that a gay athletic association existed—which is why it took me several years to find it. When I finally did and joined a team, I didn't recognize anyone on any of the teams: I had never encountered them at bookstore programs, coffeehouse events, or women's music concerts. Though it's likely that some of them had attended these events, they certainly weren't regulars. And when I would mention, in those days (around 1983 or 1984), that comedian Kate Clinton or poet Audre Lorde was going to be in town, I would get blank looks more often than not.

I also discovered, after some time, that the jocks were kind of afraid of me—or at least afraid to talk around me. Because they knew I was active outside of sports, many perceived me as some sort of raging, politically correct feminist. As a consequence, my teammates feared that with the least amount of provocation on their part or at the slightest political error in speech, I would start berating them. Thankfully, this has changed a bit over the years. My teammates know that although there are certain jokes I don't find funny, and that I have definite opinions about a lot of things concerning our community, I seldom get up on a soapbox and begin ranting at them. And for my part, I have continued to advertise cultural events to them—and occasionally they actually attend.

This closing of the ranks is becoming more prevalent overall. I am no longer the only person I know of in the league, to give one example, who is active in lesbian cultural events. More of the jocks have been showing up at the Michigan Womyn's Music Festival, and there were many who either went or very much wanted to go to the 1987 Gay and Lesbian March on Washington.

This is heartening on a number of levels. Personally, I no longer feel like a solitary bridge between the two parts of the community, having to explain and defend each half to the other. Both seem to have greater knowledge, acceptance, and understanding. But more important than making me feel more comfortable, this interaction indicates a growing sense of unity—something that is critical when you're part of an oppressed minority. The intermixing helps encourage jocks to examine the habits of language and behavior that they may have been accepting unquestioned, until now, and it helps give feminists a new appreciation of the special brand of homophobia confronting athletic women.

While on the one hand it is unrealistic to suggest that all members of each part of the community embrace the activities of the other as their own, on the other hand, it's important to all of us that we support one another—even if this amounts to nothing more than recognizing that *both* jocks and feminists are more talented and capable than generally given credit. What we've tended to lose sight of sometimes is that neither the jocks nor the feminists are, on their own, the real lesbian community. Each is a different aspect of the same, rich personality that makes up our lesbian world. Both contribute to our lesbian heritage and tradition; both have something to learn from one another; and both are necessary, integral parts of the whole. The real lesbian community is made up of jocks *and* feminists—and every shade of dyke in between.

Notes

1. From "Soapbox" (letters to the editor), *Hot Wire: A Journal of Women's Music and Culture* 4, no. 1 (November 1987): 7.

2. Linn ni Cobhan, "Lesbians in Physical Education and Sport," in *Lesbian Studies: Present and Future*, ed. Margaret Cruikshank (Old Westbury, N.Y.: Feminist Press, 1982), p. 181.

3. Ed Zolna and Mike Conklin, *Mastering Softball* (Chicago: Contemporary Books, Inc., 1981); and *Miller Lite Report on Women in Sports* (New York: Women's Sports Foundation, 1985).

4. In Janis L. Taylor (director and producer), *When Diamonds Were a Girl's Best Friend: The 1986 Reunion of the All-American Girls Baseball League* (Chicago, 1987), video documentary.

5. Mary A. Boutilier and Lucinda SanGiovanni, *The Sporting Woman* (Champaign, Ill.: Human Kinetics Publishers, 1983), p. 47.

6. Kate Clinton, "Making Light: Notes on Feminist Humor," *Trivia: A Journal of Ideas*, vol. 1 (Fall 1982).

7. Yvonne Zipter, "Making Conversation with Kate Clinton," *Hot Wire: A Journal of Women's Music and Culture* 1, no. 1 (November 1984): 14.

8. Quoted in Michele Kort, "*Ms.* Conversation," *Ms.* (February 1988), pp. 61-62.

9. Lynn Rossellini, "Homosexuals in Sports: Lesbians and Straights," *New York Post*, December 13, 1975.

10. Boutilier and SanGiovanni, pp. 45-46.

11. Rita Mae Brown, *A Plain Brown Rapper* (Oakland, Calif.: Diana Press, 1976), p. 222.

12. *Miller Lite Report on Women in Sports*, p. 15.

13. Cobhan, p. 183.

14. Rita Mae Brown, "Take a Lesbian to Lunch," in her *A Plain Brown Rapper*, p. 83.

15. Boutilier and SanGiovanni, p. 120.

Chapter 8

Keeping Score: How's Softball Doing Against The "Isms"?

Most of us, at some time in our lives, have had the experience of feeling different, of being the "odd ball" in a group—the only woman, the only person of color, the oldest or youngest person, the only lesbian. The experience of differentness, depending on the others involved and our own approach to the situation, can be positive or negative. We can end up feeling good about our uniqueness, or like outcasts.

One could expect that softball teams, as products of this culture, would simply reflect society's attitudes concerning otherness, and that its players would react in the same way as anyone else in the society—sometimes well and sometimes (perhaps all too often) badly. To some degree this is true. But softball has a way of creating an atmosphere that is special in its ability to bring people together. Does this unifying quality cut through boundaries between races? Between the sexes? Between different generations? Between lesbians and heterosexual women? Can playing softball together break down the stereotypes

different groups have of one another? Or are the stereotypes simply reinforced?

Race
On Dividing—And Not Always Conquering Racism

Pat Parker: "Unfortunately, being a softball player does
not mean that one has done the work they need to do
in terms of racism, sexism, whatever. . . . Several years
ago, when I played on bar teams, the racism was so bad
that I and a group of women formed an organization
called *Gente* (which is, literally translated, *people* in
Spanish). And the reason we did that was because there
was an incident. This [was] a bar league; we played softball, then basketball. There was a point, actually during one of the basketball games, when one woman on
my team called a woman on a friend of mine's team a
"nigger." Now that didn't make *me* feel very good, and
of course, it didn't make the woman on the other team
feel O.K. either. And we met afterwards, sat down and
talked about 'Now what do we do with this? Here we
are, playing our hearts out with these people, and we
can't be sure of them.' What we did was we formed a
team that was only for Third World women. It created
such a furor here. People assumed, first, based on the
stereotype that Women of Color are better athletes,
that we would dominate the league. Secondly, they assumed that if we lost—*or* if we won—we would probably beat up the people we played. I think they probably thought we were running around with switchblades
and chains in our shorts. And it was really almost
comical—if it hadn't been so pathetic—to watch the
reaction. It was like people were scared to death of
what *Gente* meant and what it represented. And it was

all coming from those stereotypes. I don't know if it's gotten better because I've pretty much divorced myself from a lot of areas."[1]

Mei: "Racism is so subtle. . . . [And sometimes] I don't notice because I'm suppressing it. I know that there must have been some in Iowa and Minnesota where I grew up. But I haven't really thought about it. . . . I do know that I always thought I had to be better than anybody, than any of the white people—I was mostly on white teams and I was usually the only nonwhite—and I felt like I sort of had to bat for the whole Chinese race. . . . [I felt like] I had to be exceptional to be accepted on the team. Maybe that was more something that I put on [myself], but that's something I felt throughout all my softball playing."

Florence: "I was at a party at a hotel once [during a tournament], and a comment was made about my race that I overheard. But that could be at any party. I don't think that was associated with softball."

Olivia: "Most of the teams around here are, for the most part, segregated. You have basically a lot of white women playing together. So therefore you don't usually have a racial situation there. And a lot of Third World women like to form teams together. So that's O.K. But the times I can think of when there have been mixed teams—not 100 percent of the time, but I can't think of that many examples of mixed teams—but when I do I can usually come up with racial incidents. . . . When I think of the racial incidents that have happened, they're not always overtly hostile things. And I think in some cases, it's kind of a catalyst to educate people. . . . People on my team have said [racist] things

to me and they're all pretty well-educated women, but they're ignorant about certain things."

As Pat Parker says, "Being a softball player does not mean that one has done the work they need to do in terms of racism." In fact, there are those who maintain that as nonfeminists, predominantly, softball players have *definitely* not done the necessary antiracism work. But that's an overstatement. For one thing, not all softball dykes are nonfeminists, and not all feminists are engaged in struggling against racism. In any case, there are a lot of softball players (feminist or not) who *have* been working on challenging the ways in which racism is perpetuated. The give and take of softball can be very helpful in this process.

But racist incidents such as the one Pat Parker described continue to occur. Though that specific encounter took place in the mid-seventies, such travesties based on stereotypes, are still perpetuated. Here in Chicago, for instance, as recently as the early 1980s, white teams in the lesbian basketball league expressed fears that the incoming Black teams would dominate the league because of their (assumed) greater experience and "natural" abilities in the game. Though this illustration comes from basketball, not softball, it is unfortunately clear that racial stereotypes persist in athletics.

On a more positive note, however, I have found that a repeated refusal to let racist comments go unnoticed lessens their occurrence. And as Olivia pointed out, in some cases such situations or comments can be kind of a catalyst to educate people. More often than not, though, there seems to be little opportunity for any interaction between Women of Color and white women, positive *or* negative, because most teams are not well-integrated.

Segregated Softball

Judy Thompson: "There aren't very many Black women that are gay playing softball [in this league]. In our league last year there were three. . . . And Mexicans, there were maybe that many. And the rest were all white."

Linda Locke: "Lately, in the time I've been playing since I've been out, I've been real fortunate to be on teams that were predominantly lesbians of color. . . . So the women are very aware and political. . . . Playing in high school and playing on other teams [than the Women of Color teams], I noticed being the only person of color. . . . But most recently I don't notice that as much. The thing I do notice is that at lesbian softball games, most of the teams there are white teams. I think that in the lesbian community there are just a lot of white women."

V.: "In our twelve-inch [softball] league there's very few [other] Black women. . . . It doesn't make me uncomfortable; it just makes me wonder. In fact I can count three on my hand. . .or four. That's about it. And I know Black women like to play softball."

Celeste Methot: "I have to admit that most of the teams [in Atlanta] did not have very many Black women on them. As a matter of fact, the *majority* of teams did not have any Black women on them. I played with one team three years, and it wasn't until last year that we had one Black woman on it."

Pat Parker: "The team I play on [now] has two Black women on it, three Chicanas, one Asian, and the rest pretty much white. And ours is the most racially mixed team in the league. In fact, this year, this season, is the first time I've ever seen another Black woman play on a team in this area."

Mary Farmer: "There is not nearly as much integration of the teams as I would like to see myself, but there are tons of Black women's softball teams, some dyke, some not."

Florence: "I think there's probably a lot of cultural difference in general. We were one of the first Blacks to move into the area I live in, so I grew up in an all-mixed environment. So I'm the type of person where I feel comfortable around different people. . . . I think a lot of problems with a lot of Black women in particular is that maybe the culture that they were raised into, they don't feel comfortable with anyone outside of their own race, and they sort of isolate themselves even though you may have a common bond of being gay, you're still isolating yourself. And I think that's the biggest barrier, people not wanting to experience one another and just sticking in their own groups. . . . Although over five or six years I have seen where there have been a lot more Black women athletes participating in rugby, softball, and basketball. It's sort of a good feeling. I like to see that. Because I think it's a step of uniting all the way over."

The racist ideas that people possess often come from having little or no *real* contact with the other race in question. Almost without exception, women report that few Women of Color play in the same leagues or on the same teams that white women do. That's true in Chicago, too. (Though, perhaps encouragingly, the number of Black women in the league I play in doubled or tripled over the course of a year; unfortunately, the population of other Women of Color ballplayers remained small.) In some areas, the imbalance between whites and Women of Color is reasonable because the general population of that area is also very white. But in areas that are more racially mixed, both gay and nongay leagues need to examine why there are so few Women of Color playing in them.

Why Our Teams Aren't Well Mixed

Mary Farmer: "There are a lot of Black women who would say it is more difficult for them to be out in certain parts of their community and so [playing in a gay league] is not something they rush to do."

Olivia: "[The segregation of teams] has a lot to do with who you hang out with. I don't think when anybody recruits people that they recruit them based on any ethnic kind of thing. I think it's just people tend to form teams with their friends. . . . The team that I was asked to coach was a team of all white women. . . . It's not that they wouldn't play with anybody of another background. It's not anything like that at all. I just don't think they know anybody except for me. . . . It's not a conscious thing."

V.: "I know downtown there is a field on Thursday full of Black women playing softball. . . . I know all those girls on those teams aren't straight. I mean you can go out there and look for yourself and you can identify them quick. But they won't play on the MSA [gay] league. Maybe they don't want to be identified themselves. . . . I don't really know. There's a lot of Black gay women I know, that are out, who have jobs that

don't demand that [they remain closeted], who play
softball, but they don't play on the MSA team. I have
no idea [why]. [But] I know how hard it is to just go to
a different group and say, 'Hey, I want to play.' [And
yet], I don't personally think that somebody has to go
out of their way to say to somebody else, 'Hey, you can
play.' I think it's your job, if you want to participate,
to go up and find out for yourself."

Judy Thompson: "[It may be that Women of Color are
concerned about being in gay leagues.] I know the Mexicans, in their own families, it's *real* taboo to be queer.
Whereas, even though many families frown upon it—
white families—I don't think it's quite as bad. I have
Mexican friends who would never ever ever ever ever
tell their families because they'd be ostracized."

Rhonda Craven: "[In terms of] gay leagues, Black wom-
en in particular, and I'm sure other Women of Color,
tend to be much more closeted or less willing to be out.
I think there's also the socializing factor where it's not
necessarily looked upon well to mix socially with white
women. And since the majority of women who are playing softball are white—often you get talked about if you
socialize, if you hang out with white people too much.
So I think that's part of it also. Then I think there's also
some more rigid roles prescribed as far as what women
are and are not supposed to do [in the Black commu-
nity]. It's not ladylike and men won't put up with you
if you try to be jockish or macho, et cetera. So I think
there's a certain level of discouragement that might be
internalized (even after a Woman of Color comes out)
that she's not supposed to do this, even though there's
this part of her that probably wants to. So I think all
of those are factors why there aren't as many lesbians

of color actually playing in the leagues. Often also because any women jocks are almost automatically perceived as being lesbians or gay or something like that and a lot of people don't want to have that stigma attached to them publicly even if they are."

In addition to issues of outness, prior friendships, and comfort, the poor integration of softball teams is an inevitable mirroring of the integration patterns in our society as a whole. And while it may be true, as V. says, that "it's your job, if you want to participate, to go up and find out for yourself," it is also true that, if the previously accepted boundaries between the races are going to be broken down, women on both sides have to be committed to doing it. Even if these barriers could disintegrate on their own (not a possibility that history encourages), it would be a very long process—a process that could certainly be moved along by making an extra effort to welcome Women of Color, by wanting their participation on softball teams where white women have traditionally played.

Although it might appear reasonable that white women should also be welcomed on Women of Color teams, it is harder to make a case for this. Confronted with the dominant white society daily, Women of Color sometimes need the kind of validation they can get only from people who share their life experiences. This is true even though softball may be one place—and occasionally the only place— where a Woman of Color lesbian can go for support for both her racial experience and her lifestyle. White women need validation for their lesbianism, but seldom if ever for their racial identity.

Softball As A Bridge

Stephie: "The leagues I played in, [race] wasn't a big issue. I mean, if you wanted to play, you played. If you were good, they didn't care where you were at. I know one Black girl in particular when I was in high school, and we used to play against her, who's in the [gay] league now, and she's cool, she's alright. . .you know, you're an athlete. That's what's neat about that, you are an athlete, and there is no. . .racism when you're an athlete like that. You [both just] like to play sports."

Florence: "I'm probably one of the first Black women athletes to actually start playing a lot of competitive ball in San Diego. I remember years ago being the only Black woman playing on a team or in a league or at the nationals, for instance. But I honestly couldn't say I ever faced [racism]. At times, I may have felt uncomfortable, but, overall, people treated me as an athlete in the field. . . . I think as long as we had the common thing of playing softball, you were accepted as a player."

Barbara Grier: "Ironically. . .down here in Tallahassee, all the teams we fielded were racially mixed teams. . . this little group of women buddy around together all the time. . . . I thought it would be much more racist [here] than in the Midwest; it's not."

Jean Claiborne: "If you interact more with a person, then you're more apt to understand them. . . . That's been my experience."

Miller Lite Report on Women in Sports: Of the 1,555 women athletes surveyed, 91 percent agreed that "participation in racially mixed sports/fitness groups often reduces prejudice."[2]

Suzi: "Softball is a means to get to the attitudes and motives of individuals. It's a point of interest, a beginning to get people to know others who they ordinarily might not associate with. For example, a certain respect might develop on the field, for playing ability, competitiveness, sportsmanship, or sense of humor. This can be developed through social interactions following the game, and two minds open up to each other. Hopefully, this would expand to promote a united community."

When different racial groups *are* successfully brought together to form teams, softball can and does act as a bridge. The long hours spent in practice and playing, the shared experiences, the common goal—all of these things bring women on a team closer together. As we get to know people from other backgrounds, our stereotypes and prejudices begin to break down. This is supported by research, but is so logical that research hardly seems necessary.[3]

Any new-found specific insight concerning race may not immediately carry over to more generalized situations. We may compartmentalize our positive experience by saying, for instance, that we like this one Black woman or this one Asian woman or this one white woman, who we see as somehow different or separate from her race, as special. But even then it's a start—"a step of uniting all the way over," as Florence says. And the more racially mixed the teams and our leagues are, the better a bridge softball will become.

Gender

Beth: "Sometimes men think they need to play the positions that women are in as well as their own. It is fairly easy to dissuade them by being forthright and blunt. My experience has been that only true assholes don't listen, and they are rotten to everyone on the team —men and women alike."

Jo: "Most of the time you see male authorities degrade women players. The coaches are verbally brutal with their players, when women make errors or don't do something exactly to men's liking."[4]

Spike: "When I was a mechanic in the transportation industry in L.A. [about 1980] there were many softball players, male and female, and some were pretty serious. Some of the small number of women who worked there (all told there were about 20 women and 700 men) organized some coed softball games. But then the guys got serious and kicked the women off the teams and organized tournaments."

Mei: "I just got done playing a coed tournament . . . and that was really a different experience. But it was a good experience. The guys were really supportive. Although, I saw a lot of other teams not being as supportive, the guys robbing the ball right out of the women's gloves almost."

Toni McNaron: "Everyone agreed they much preferred a woman [for coach]. What they observed in the male coaches was a holding back of the women from developing any personal style."[5]

Suzi: "The formerly men's, now coed, team recruited me, yet some men had a hard time initially playing with a woman, especially when I would start and/or play ahead of them. This dissolved to the most extent; however, some of the new players seem a bit taken aback sometimes (depending on the person and his previous experience)."

Linda Locke: "Recently. . .I was playing on a [coed] team. I'm an outfielder. I was playing in the field, and I was playing next to this man. And it's real danger-ous. Because I think maybe they don't take you seri-ously. When I play, I always call the ball. . .because I don't want to get hurt. I got almost knocked over by him. I got the ball taken away. And it never got to the point where he would say, 'O.K., she can handle it. I don't have to go and take the ball away to get the out.' So I just got fed up. I just got tired of proving myself. I'm not real big, and he'd just run me over."

Starla Sholl: "Coed teams are always a problem for me; the men are usually overpowering (sexist), and espe-cially in straight teams, the women tend to be overly submissive."

Meryl Moskowitz: "Males tend to dominate and change the tone to competitive—not good for a semi-skilled woman player."

Florence: "I've played on a couple coed [teams]. I like the competition, but I don't like some of the attitudes that are displayed, simply because I think the men still have that macho image about playing, and I just want to go out there and play ball. So I have a slight conflict with that at times. . . . But, you know, it's the sort of sexism that's not directed. I think it's just their be-havior. I don't think they even realize it a lot of times. Because some of that attitude would normally be there even when the guys were playing against guys. It's just certain people have the attitude that they are in con-trol of everything, more so, of course, against women because they're considered weaker."

Most of us have probably had, at one time or another, similar experiences to those above. And even when the men don't realize they are behaving in a sexist manner, the behavior is no less sexist. As annoying as such behavior can be, there are real benefits to playing on coed softball teams—especially on gay coed softball teams.

The main benefit, of course, is that it brings two parts of a community—gay males and lesbians—together that often have few other opportunities to get to know one another, a phenomenon that seems particularly prevalent in major metropolitan areas where each part of the community tends to have its own discrete social circles. Even in smaller communities, where gay men and lesbians may not have multiple separate activities and gathering places to choose from, playing softball together provides an avenue for socializing and getting to know one another.

Art Johnston: "We probably have the least interplay among lesbians and gay men of any city I know. My own connection with lesbians has come through sports . . . . We have this fall co-rec league. It's small but it's very nice. . . . It's a wonderful place to see men's eyes—men who've never played ball on a field with women before and who obviously have all the male notions about this. And then you would see a really fine play [by a woman] or you would see a hit . . . . It's wonderful to watch the new respect that takes place. Because you'll see at first when the people go out on the field, the women will sort of be talking to each other. The woman at second base and the [female] left fielder will be chatting with each other. And the guys will be chatting with each other. And then after the first game, it changes. And it's one of the things I enjoy the most."

Suzi: "My activities in coed softball . . . I've got political motives. In that the gay and lesbian society is bro-

ken into two divisions, and it further separates—within those divisions. . . . And I look at softball as a means—and I've seen it grow in Milwaukee and in other cities —of accepting different male lifestyles, men accepting different women's lifestyles, and just saying, 'Hey, she's a good dyke. I like her.' Or a woman going, 'He's the cutest little faggot. I used to hate those guys'. . . . It's not healthy for the community as a whole [to be divided] . . . . I would like to think athletics—softball, bowling, volleyball—is a good way to get people to lower their defenses so they can start knowing people who are different from them."

Despite these benefits, for some women, so much of the rest of their lives—at work and in the world at large—is filled with men, that their leisure time is something they prefer to reserve specifically for women.

Jean Claiborne: "I do not enjoy playing coed. I don't particularly enjoy being around men, for one."

Bea: "[Softball] is the part of my life I give to my lesbian self, and I think I would only want to play my favorite sport with lesbian/feminists."

Obviously, it's a choice that each of us has to make individually. But if we do decide to play coed softball and can manage to stick out the initial sexism that may be present, the experience can be enlightening for both men and women. Frequently men learn nonsexist ways of interacting, and, in addition, playing together can help unify the gay and lesbian communities—a function we can't afford to undervalue.

Age

Miki Adachi: "We have a twenty-year [age] spread on our team. The youngest is twenty, the oldest is forty. The average is thirty. [And] I remember in my college days we had one player who was seventeen and another who was thirty-four—double the age. I think it's good because it adds variety."

Miki's experience seems to be the norm. If women have any particular feeling about having a wide range of ages represented on their teams, it's that it is a good experience for all involved. Age differences were never once mentioned as a problem area on softball teams.

In softball there is a unique opportunity for lesbians of different generations to socialize with one another. This in itself is valuable, as it allows lesbians who may have come out in divergent social climates to understand their various concerns and values. Furthermore, more experienced women can give support to lesbians who are just coming out and can serve as much-needed role models. In the league I play in, women range in age from their early twenties to their fifties, and I know of women in their sixties in other cities who still play ball. While some teams tend to group themselves by age—there are "younger" and "older" teams—the age range of a given team is often considerable, spanning ten, fifteen, or twenty years.

Sexual Preference

Susan Begg: "[The] straight women [on the team were] upset/embarrassed by lesbians being out in public, afraid it would reflect on them."

Jean Claiborne: "I've been on teams with ladies that were married . . . and I'm obviously very gay. I don't flaunt it, but I just don't think I look like the average feminine woman—I guess I'm about as close to a dyke as you can get. [The straight women] just don't care, I don't think. I mean if they cared, they wouldn't be [there]. . . . We were just out there playing softball. I think there's almost a prejudice the other way. . . like, after the game we wanted to go to the bar or something. . .and if most of the team is gay, it's harder to have two or three straight people on the team because then you start tending to act like a gay group. . . . You don't want them to feel uncomfortable, but then you don't want someone to spoil how you want to be. It hampers your fun because then you have to kind of keep yourself in check the whole time as far as what you say, how you act. Also, when you're in a situation where you're in a majority of gay people and one or two straights, you do forget and you think, 'Well, God—that makes them feel pretty shitty or bad or uncomfortable for Chrissakes'. . . . The team I'm on now is all gay, and it's just a lot easier because you don't have to worry about it."

Joan Bender: "My assistant coach [when acting as our coach] treated me like shit cuz he knew I was gay. I sat on the bench because he said he didn't like my attitude. He would make crude comments behind my back."

Laurie: "A few teams [I was on] were homophobic—as if [being a lesbian] really determines how good you are or what type of person! (I was pretty closeted at the time, so I wasn't the focus of their jeers.)"

Dorothy Kidd: "Sally thinks [the closeted lesbianism on the team] led to the male coach cutting a veteran player at the spring try-outs because she brought her 'openly gay' friends to watch."[6]

Melinda Shaw: "I had problems with two different teams which had closeted lesbians and, mostly, straight women whose husbands coached. They got upset when I showed outward signs of affection at a field while watching another game [and] subsequently ignored me, stopped playing me much and, when I was put in, would say things like 'Now let's see if you can do anything' and tried to intimidate me while I was batting. I quit both teams."

Stephie: "When I was playing in park district leagues, when I was younger, you'd hear stories about, 'Oh that woman over there—see her?—she's a [lesbian].' And I was thinking to myself, 'Jeez, what do they think about me?' "

R. J.: "A straight woman on the team I played for last year was kind of violent in her views about gays. She had heard the talk about me and absolutely did not want me to play on the same team she did—the other players talked her into giving me a chance and trying not to come down too hard on me. So. . . I started playing on the team. She wouldn't even stay in the dugout when I was in there and never had anything friendly to say to me. Then due to extenuating circumstances she got 'stuck' riding to a weekend tournament with me and another woman who is bisexual, it was approximately a five-hour drive one way. The bisexual and I expressed our views and talked openly like the other gal wasn't even there. . . . Finally things started calming down with this straight gal, and she began feeling more comfortable around 'us.' At the end-of-the-season softball party she said to me in front of all the other players: 'R. J., I've got to apologize to you for my attitude toward you this year. I did not want you to play on this team at all, but I learned you're not like what I thought you would be. You're a good person. . . . You simply have different views and desires than me, I sure hope you'll play with us next year.' I couldn't believe it! I wish everyone could be that open and honest. I guess she thought I'd be some kind of nympho and attack anything with tits—I don't know. There needs to be an awareness [in] people who don't understand. . . . And there are a lot of people who don't—especially in rural, middle America."

It's not really surprising that many straight women have such a strong negative reaction to lesbians. Given that most women in team sports are assumed to be lesbians whether they are or not, and given that lesbianism is not generally considered something desirable outside of the homosexual community, many straight women, in an effort to make it clear that *they* are not lesbians, and to protect themselves from the negative consequences of being considered a lesbian, go out of their way to disparage women who *are* lesbians. Occasionally, and even more sadly, there are closeted lesbians who, to divert attention and speculation from themselves, will put down openly gay players.

Heterosexual women may not welcome us immediately with open arms—and the most homophobic among them may never welcome us at all—but extended contact with them is bound to break down barriers. It is not always advisable or possible to be out, of course, but when we can be who we are, progress is made—no matter how painfully slow sometimes. As Sharon Guthrie discovered in her research, it is lack of information or knowledge that perpetuates homophobia, and "the more exposure people have to accurate information about homosexuality, the more tolerant their attitudes."[7]

Overall, then, softball can be an unintended tool for dismantling many stereotypes and for building bridges between previously separate groups. As such, softball is given short shrift when referred to as "just a game." Clearly, it's more than that.

Notes

1. For another account of *Gente*, see "We Have To Be Our Own Spark: Interview with 'Gente' Third-World Lesbian Softball Team," *Lesbian Tide* 3, no. 11 (July 1974).

2. *Miller Lite Report on Women in Sports* (New York: Women's Sports Foundation, 1985).

3. See, e.g., Alfie Kohn, "It's Hard to Get Left Out of a Pair," *Psychology Today* (October 1987), p. 54.

4. Toni McNaron, "An Interview with the Wilder Ones," *So's Your Old Lady*, no. 10 (September 1975), p. 8.

5. McNaron, p. 8.

6. Dorothy Kidd, "Dyke Dynamos: Women in Sports," *Pink Ink* (Toronto) (August 1983), p. 15.

7. Michele Kort, "High Marks for Homophobia," *Women's Sports* (November 1982), p. 54.

Chapter 9

Brought To You By...
A Word About
Our Sponsors

The tradition of softball team sponsorship is a long one, stretching at least as far back as the days of the first industrial leagues. "By 1938, sponsorship of women's softball teams had been taken up by banks, bakeries, restaurants, ice creameries, truck lines and businesses of all sorts. It didn't take long for businesses to discover that sponsorship of men's and women's softball teams was a cheap, effective advertising source."[1] Before the days of TV and other readily available entertainments, softball games were very well-attended, and sponsoring a team was indeed a good, inexpensive way to advertise.

While this is still the case in some areas of the country—both that softball games are well-attended and that, therefore, team sponsorship continues to be effective advertising—in other places, softball games are seldom watched by anyone other than the players and a few of their friends and loved ones. Even in the latter case, team sponsorship is still prevalent, though less for advertising purposes than for reasons such as good will or the expectation of patronage by the team itself.

Team sponsorship has changed in other ways as well over the years. While there continue to be various types of sponsors (depending on the specifics of the city, town, or softball league), one category of sponsor is most prevalent: bars. Bar sponsorship brings with it auxiliary phenomena that are worth considering, including how sponsorship intersects with another long-standing softball tradition—beer drinking—and how sponsorship can result in a special relationship between sponsor and team.

It is quite possible to play league softball without a sponsor, of course. Some leagues, in fact, are *traditionally* sponsorless, but sponsors can make it possible for many women to play who might otherwise not be able to. In leagues where sponsors are the norm, sponsors also help give a team a sense of identity and belonging.

Because of the important role sponsors can play in the life of a team, team sponsorship is an integral part of the dyke softball phenomenon.

Who Are They?

Barbara Grier (Naiad Press, Publisher): "Garages, bars, restaurants, machine shops . . . blue-collar businesses, blue-collar world. That's the kind of people. Now, there are some exceptions. Big business, like all over Kansas City, all of the big, mainstream, important businesses, i.e., 'when you care enough to send the very best' Hallmark, BMA—Businessmen Assurance Company—one of the largest insurance underwriters in the country, all of those businesses. The big banks, they all had teams too. Those teams are likely to be a bit more spit and polish, though, and a little less clearly dykey."

Other commonly mentioned sponsors include everything from women's bookstores to construction companies, from lesbian-owned cafés to livestock salebarns—as well as camper and car dealerships, printers, vending machine companies, and mini-marts. Businesses that are not woman- or gay-owned are generally the sponsors of teams in conventional leagues, such as park district leagues or straight bar leagues—often unaware of or turning an unseeing eye to the fact that many of the women on the team are lesbians. Whereas, in leagues that are specifically gay and lesbian, the sponsors are generally also gays and lesbians—and more often than not, this means bars.

Art Johnston (Sponsor): "The teams that I know of across the country in the [North American Gay Amateur Athletic Alliance] are mostly bar-sponsored."

Women's bars, men's bars, mixed bars—bars were mentioned as sponsors more than any other type of business by softball dykes from coast to coast. At first glance, it seems obvious why bars sponsor teams: to encourage team members to patronize their establishment. But what about men's bars that sponsor women's teams? Or teams whose members are mostly nondrinkers? What prompts bars to lend support in those cases? As for the other types of businesses, while a few (like restaurants) might also reasonably be able to expect some patronage from their team, many can expect little or no monetary remuneration from the teams they sponsor. So why do they do it?

Why Do They Sponsor Us?

Judy Thompson (Printer): "I have no revenue coming in [from] sponsoring a team. It's like, who's going to go get something printed? Whereas [with] a bar, the team

can always go drink and pay back the guy for putting up the money for the entry fee."

Often, as I've already pointed out, bars can't even expect to be compensated for their sponsorship. But there are any number of other reasons why businesses choose to put up their hard-earned money to give lesbians the opportunity to play softball.

Mary Farmer (Lammas Bookstore): "I sponsor a team because I think lesbian sports are important. . . . And I think it's important that lesbian bookstores do as much as they can, which sometimes is not a lot, monetarily, because they don't have a lot of extra resources . . . . [But] we [should] do as much as we can to put ourselves back into the community."

Art Johnston (Sidetrack, Men's Bar): It was as much out of good will as trying to raise money, [though] the women's teams were supportive in the way that they could be, which was after a game [they'd come in] or whatever. . . . When [the women's division of the gay league] started growing, our tradition in the sports association was sponsorship by bars because it began as a kind of softball beer league, which has happened in most of the gay associations across the country. And when this happened, we were sitting at a board meeting of the sports association saying, 'How are we going to handle this? We have a major influx of women, and we don't have, number one, enough women's bars [to sponsor them] or women's bars with a tradition of sponsoring these teams.' (Probably because of the difference in socializing. The role of going out to the bars, drinking, and spending a lot of money—men do that more than women do. Partly it's economic factors, partly because I think the dating habits are different.) So we said, 'Why does it have to be a women's bar?' And fortunately, at the time, we had extremely good business at Sidetrack, and it was very easy for us to do that. And a number of other men's bars jumped into it."

Mei: "[One] sponsor we had strictly wanted the exposure —he just wanted us to bring in the trophies."

Mary Azzano (RSVP & Co., Restaurant): "The ladies were customers and just in a conversation one night—I knew they had a baseball team—they had lost their sponsor, which was the Lady Bug [a now-defunct women's bar], and I asked them who was going to sponsor them. They said they were going to look for a straight bar. I said [to myself], 'Well there are enough gay businesses to support gay teams.' So I did it . . . . Basically, [I just wanted to] give back some of the money into the community."

Carrie (Lost and Found, Women's Bar): "[We've] been sponsoring teams here for years. . . . It's the same kids. As a matter of fact, one team [we've] been sponsoring for five or six years. They're the same regular customers that come into the bar. And then this year, [we] sponsored [another team], which was a new team . . . . It's mostly good will."

Although even bars don't seem to be "in it for the money," for every softball dyke who isn't a drinker or a bar-goer, there are probably at least two more who are. And with the long marriage between baseball/softball and beer, most bars that sponsor a team can expect a fair amount of business from their team.

Susan Begg: "The sport where there's always seemed to be the most drinking has always been softball. And I think that, at least here in Ithaca, many of the bars do sponsor teams, both men's and women's teams. The feeling has been, since they're our sponsors, first of all, that's a natural place to go celebrate after a game. In other words, if the team plans to go meet as a team and have a few beers after the game, then they're naturally going to their sponsor's bar. And the feeling, I think, is also that since they are the sponsors, [we] should support them and give them some business."

Missy Myers: "The negative aspect [of playing on dyke teams] has been the emphasis on the bars and alcohol, which I don't mind occasionally but which is pretty obsessive with some teams I've been with."

Initially, I was concerned that bar sponsorship might somehow subtly encourage drinking. But in fact it seems more likely that if the women on a team are going to drink, they're going to drink, and if not, not—bar sponsor or no.

Stephie: "Alcohol has always been a factor, especially [with] softball games. . . . I don't drink anymore; I quit drinking about three and a half years ago. But . . .you have to go to the bar, you have to support them. [But] they drink, a lot of the gals, before the game, during the game, after the game. I don't think I ever did that. And it wasn't very big on my team either, the team I played with. But on the other teams, yes, that's the thing. It's like a bar night only during the day. They're out to have fun, you know. . .'Let's get the cooler.' And that was, I think, the whole league. That was summertime: you bring out the cooler. . . . I think being sponsored by a bar *does* help. I mean, being sponsored by a restaurant you just may get fed. I can't see people bringing coolers of sandwiches over [though] instead of beer. No matter who you're sponsored by, they're going to drink. That's just the thing to do. Softball, hot day, beer. I don't think being sponsored by a bar matters."

Susan Begg: "I think it's true that, whether you have a bar sponsoring you or not, certain teams—at least what I would call 'drinking teams'—will go to the bar regardless. . . . I think softball is, from my experience, a prime sport for that and that's because it's a summer sport. People get hot and sweaty, and drinking beer seems to be a natural."

Barbara Grier: "I think alcohol abuse. . .might be slightly exaggerated [in the lesbian community]—now that's. . .just a guess. . . . A lot of the groups of women on the teams don't drink at all. Even if they maybe are sponsored by a bar. And maybe if half the team goes, religiously, after the game to a particular bar to hang out where they eat pizza and drink beer—I think they go to these places to eat as much as not. . . . It's insane [to connect bar sponsorship and drinking]. It's almost like saying, 'If your team is sponsored by a barbecue rib place, you would eat nothing but barbeque ribs.' Or, 'If your team' (even more fun), 'is sponsored by a garage, would you drink gasoline?' So I don't think there's necessarily a correlation."

Celeste Methot: "My team has never had the benefit of full sponsorship. But a lot of teams that have sponsors, their sponsors provide cases and cases of beer after the tournament or the game (not mostly games though). There've been plenty of times where I've seen teams, just out in the parking lot sitting in the back of a pick-up truck, slugging down beers in between games. Drinking is a real big part of it. It hasn't been for me so much, although I cherish that after-a-game beer, especially when it's hot outside. There are a lot of especially younger women that drink immense amounts. And you can always count on the fact that, if there's a large softball tournament in town, like a national tournament or one of the major tournaments, if you are in a city where there are women's bars, you can count on those bars being packed on a Saturday night [with softball players]."

Art Johnston: "There are bars which view themselves entirely as places to get loaded, in a real old-time sense, you know, [where] the point of a bar is to get yourself falling down drunk. And when that's the case, teams that end up playing there seem to be that way. . . . The [women's] team that we sponsor, they had said to me in the beginning, 'We want you to know that there are a lot of people on the team who are in AA.' And I said, 'I don't have any problem with that. That doesn't matter.' And it hasn't mattered [to me as a sponsor]. So I think it is the specific bar."

Having a bar sponsor certainly doesn't do anything to *discourage* drinking, but then, discouraging consumption of alcohol is neither the responsibility of the bar nor the sponsor's role. Their primary role is, of course, to pay the fees and, perhaps, provide uniforms. This is no small contribution. Fees vary greatly from league to league, but amounts in the hundreds are not uncommon. The fee for Chicago's gay league, for instance, has been $350 per team, which covers diamond rental from the park district, insurance, and umpires. The cost of uniforms, too, can differ drastically, depending on whether uniforms are defined as matching T-shirts, or they include everything from baseball caps down to the stirrups. This can represent an investment of anywhere from $100 to $500 per team. In addition to this kind of financial commitment, sponsors are often supportive in other ways as well.

Our Sponsors—And Us

Carrie (Lost and Found, Women's Bar): "We have a very good relationship. As a matter of fact, [we're] having a beer bust for the two teams Sunday and hot dogs and all that. It's more than just putting up the money and having your name saying you're sponsoring. . . . I was their first base coach. It's exciting. And the kids get a big kick out of it. And most of the teams come back to the bar afterwards and have a party."

Linda Locke: "One sponsor I had was the lover of one of the players. And she's an attorney in private practice. . . . [The sponsor of my other team], that woman owns a deli. She's an Asian woman. She used to be a P.E. teacher for about ten years. . . . They're friends of ours that we've asked, who happen to be in the position of having the money to sponsor us. So they have more of a role [than just providing money]. They come to our games, hang out with us afterwards."

Art Johnston: "[My relationship with the team] has varied from year to year. In the first couple of years, especially, I was very supportive and was at almost all the games. And when they got into championship situations or playoffs and things I would coach first base. . . . I continue to be perhaps overly cautious about how to participate. . . needing to be sure that they want me there—that I'm not just pushing my way

in because I'm the guy who paid the money. And sometimes I end up standing back too far from it. [But] I
could not be happier about the relationships [with the
women on the team] that have developed."

Mei: "[My team] had one sponsor who was a million-
aire. He provided us with uniforms, all the money we
needed; he came to some of our tournaments and games
and videotaped them. He was the wildest guy. I don't
know why he was interested in us. We were all gay.
You'd think he'd get the hint. I don't know. . . [I guess]
he just liked women's sports, supporting women's sports."

Mary Azzano: "I was real appreciative of the fact that
they did support the restaurant. I was very happy
about that. Therefore, I would try to support them as
much as possible. I would try to get out to as many
games as I could."

One of the owners of Piggens Pub in Chicago seems to
be the epitome of this greater level of commitment, coming to every game, bringing a large cooler of Gatorade for
the team, keeping score and/or coaching a base, having
the games videotaped, and showing the videos at her bar
after the game. These video showings are often in conjunc-
tion with a barbecue, provided by the bar for the Piggens'
team, the opposing team, and, not infrequently, another
straggling team or two. Piggens has done such a good job
of supporting women's athletics that what was once
predominantly a men's bar is now a mixed bar—especially
on weekends, when our league's games are played. In return, many of the team members make it a point to celebrate the birthdays of the bar owners and staff, and there
is always a special gift at the end of the season for the
sponsor to show the team's appreciation.

Financial support may be the most obvious role of a sponsor, but it is not the only one. It's not even necessarily the one that is most significant to a team.

A Team Of One's Own

Team sponsorship is the rule, but like every rule I know of, there are exceptions to it. Occasionally, a whole league is involved, such as the Tri-County League in the Amherst area of Massachusetts. More usually, a single team or two within a league is without a sponsor. Sometimes this is a conscious decision. Such seems to be the case with one team in Oakland, of which player Nan O'Connor says—not without a note of pride—"We are the only self-sponsored team in our league." But often, being sponsorless simply indicates the unavailability of sponsors.

Depending on the structure of the league, the latter circumstance can be a less than happy one—and not because of the financing. In the league I play in, a sponsor lends some sense of identity and prestige to its team. My team, in its various configurations (from softball to volleyball), has traditionally had difficulty in finding a sponsor and so frequently goes without one. For years we felt like the league orphans. But I think we're beginning to adjust and decide that being sponsorless isn't so bad. For instance, we realized that if we split the fee, it comes to about twenty dollars per person—less than it would cost for a night out at Paris Dance (our classiest women's bar). And in 1987, for an extra ten dollars each, we were able to get complete uniforms, which someone on the team had gotten a deal on. We have also realized that not having a sponsor (most of which are bars in our league) leaves us free to go to a bar or not after our games. And when we don't go to a bar, impromptu picnics and parties are not uncommon: we create our own fun.

This sort of autonomy is one reason why teams may make a conscious choice to be sponsorless. Autonomy can also be at issue beyond where one spends her after-game hours. Some sponsors want control over who is on the team's roster, each game's line-up, how practices are run, and so on. Another reason for choosing to self-sponsor has to do with patronage expectations on the part of sponsors, particularly bar owners. It seems fair for bar-owner sponsors to expect patronage from their teams, usually just following a game, but there are sponsors who expect substantially more than that. One potential sponsor that we talked to about sponsoring us wanted us to commit to coming in two or three nights a week! That was one time we decided we'd rather do without.

Finally, in areas of the country where gay and lesbian bars are essentially the only sponsors available, teams may also opt to self-sponsor. One woman, Fran, said that where she lives in Clearwater, Florida, the widespread homophobia makes it unwise to advertise one's association with such an establishment, and so women are reluctant to emblazon a gay bar's name on their T-shirts.

All in all, having sponsors may be traditional for women's softball teams, but being self-sponsored is also characteristic of softball dykes: it demonstrates the spirit of independence that made it possible for us to pursue a sport that, defined as unfeminine, we were generally not encouraged to play.

Notes

1. Merrie A. Fidler, "The Establishment of Softball as a Sport for American Women, 1900-1940," in *Her Story in Sport*, ed. Reet Howell (West Point, N.Y.: Leisure Press, 1982), p. 535.

Chapter 10

Wait 'Til Next Year: The Future Of Dyke Softball

When a relationship endures for an extended period of time, there is a tendency to take it for granted. It's not necessarily that we don't love the other in that relationship but, rather, more that we may not appreciate the relationship's significance or spend time contemplating why—or in what ways—it is so important. That's what it's like with softball: most of us have had a long and wonderful relationship with the game but have never really stopped to think what its deeper meaning is in our individual lives—let alone in the life of our community as a whole.

I suspect that for my part, I would have continued that way indefinitely—loving but never sufficiently valuing softball. The stories collected here from women across the nation and across time, though, have given me a new appreciation of softball's importance. I've known for quite a while that wherever you went, there were lesbians playing softball and loving it, and that it was an unparalleled meeting ground. But I don't think I knew just how deep the feelings could run or how much softball has to teach us.

Before my work on this book, while I would certainly not have dismissed the lesbian softball tradition, now I am firmly convinced that this is an institution and set of traditions worth preserving aggressively. For one thing, softball is a key unifying factor in our community. It brings together women who might otherwise have no connection with any sort of lesbian community (whether because of inclination or lack of options); it puts jocks and athletically inclined feminists together on a limited but hopefully growing basis; and it is capable of bridging racial and class barriers—as well as barriers between lesbians and gay men and between lesbians and straight women. It further helps unify us by offering rare opportunities for teamwork, cooperation, and camaraderie. And beyond providing a foundation for interconnecting some diverse parts of our community, softball is just plain and simple a healthy way to interact—and healthy in both the physical *and* mental senses of the word.

Being the ambitious sort of dyke I am, though, I'm not entirely content with keeping things just the way they are. There are a number of changes I would like to see take place in dyke softball, and in women's sports in general. Some of what I dream about for us seems quite possible; other things, while certainly not *im*possible, seem less likely to happen in any foreseeable future. But that's the great thing about dreams: they need not be constrained by present realities. Besides, reality is malleable: if enough of us have the same dream and work toward it in whatever ways we're able, reality can be reshaped.

The Women's Sports Dream
Sports For Girls

Let's start at the beginning—just like the boys get to. That is, little girls should not only be *allowed* to play Little League baseball, but they should be *encouraged* to play as well. Though I know that some girls are now playing on Little League teams, they aren't receiving the enthusiastic prompting to pursue this sport—or the quality coaching if they do play—that boys of comparable age and skill levels do. Sadly, part of this is still founded on concerns about the appropriateness of team sports for girls. In addition, as part of a vicious circle, there isn't the likelihood of returns on an investment in a baseball future for girls that there is for boys: why bother really working with little girls on their baseball skills when their career options in that area are nonexistent. And, of course, we'll never be able to enter the world of professional sports as now established until we get the necessary training.

Which is precisely the next thing I'd like to see changed: team sport opportunities for girls shouldn't stop after Little League, and girls shouldn't automatically be channeled into something more ladylike, such as tennis, gymnastics, or skating. (Those sports are great for the girls and young women whose hearts are there, but they shouldn't have to be chosen solely because there are no other options.) Currently, when girls do have opportunities to continue playing ball, it's softball, not baseball. There is no logical reason for this. If girls were given the same training and encouragement that boys receive, there would be many among them who would attain similar skill levels at every stage: Little League, high school, college, semi-pro, and professional baseball.

Well, there's the dream part, you're saying. What's the connection with reality? A little tenuous at the moment, I'll admit, but not as tenuous as it once was—which gives me, for one, hope. For instance, *no* girls used to get to play on official Little League teams before; now some do. I have no illusions that progress from here will be swift. Sport is one of the few sacrosanct male rites of passage to remain roughly intact and, as psychologist Ruth Bennett has pointed out, "Protection of sport from the intrusion of women is as critical to the power structure as is the protection of the church from Heretics."[1] Nevertheless, there are things we can do.

The first is, we can share our knowledge and love of the game with our daughters, our nieces, and the other young girls in our lives. The more that girls are exposed to the exhilaration of physical exertion and competence and to athletic female role models, the less likely they are to passively give up softball and baseball. The greater the number of voices that are raised, the harder it is to ignore the injustice—or to disregard those voices as aberrant. Social pressure may not change things overnight, but if it is persistent, it *does* change things. If we join in supporting the young women in our lives in their pursuit of athletic excellence and equality of opportunity, we will make a difference.

It would also be helpful to work for change within the systems as they now exist—the systems in question being education and Little League competition (and comparable organizations). In other words, teachers should exert as much pressure for change as they can without jeopardizing their own positions, and those others of us who are so inclined and have the opportunity should get involved in Little League as coaches or advisors. Both of these are uphill battles: education systems are generally bureaucratic and, therefore, naturally resistant to change, and Little League is still essentially a male bastion of control not likely to welcome female assistance outside of sewing numbers on uniforms or running bake sales to raise money for equipment. Yet any toehold we can get will edge us toward fulfilling our dream of someday seeing women play professional ball again. More important, it may help a young girl fulfill her dream of *playing* professional ball.

Getting On Base With Pro Baseball For Women

Instilling a love of the game, teaching the skills, and creating opportunities at the amateur level are only part of the battle, of course. *Many* women have loved baseball/softball over the years and many of them have shown considerable skill. Neither fact has made it possible for women either to play alongside men on their teams or to find support when they have formed their own teams (not, at any rate, since the AAGPBL during the late 1940s and early 1950s). So in addition to changes at the Little League and other amateur levels, what also needs to change are the following: (1) we need to be taken seriously as athletes, (2) we need to receive sufficient and appropriate media attention, (3) if we are going to be involved on a coed basis, certain rules of play and of competition may need to be revised, and (4) we need to redefine what constitutes masculine and feminine behaviors.

Serious Business

•"The stands were packed with men fans anxious to glimpse the pitchers's curves. But they couldn't very well overlook the first baseman. She was quite lovely, too. In fact, all the players were attractive during the 36th annual National Women's Softball tourney at Stratford, Conn."

•"Marlene Piper evidently intends to smack one next time up as she put on lipstick in the Raybestos team dugout."

•"Carol Spanks streaks down to first as though she had just spotted a bargain sale."[2]

These are the kinds of attitudes we're fighting. Though these particular remarks were made in 1968 and probably would not be printed today in a major metropolitan newspaper as they were then, the attitudes are still with us. Equally blatant "wit" is evident yet in small town publications and in informal banter among male friends. Even on network television, though they may not be aware of the effect of their words, sportscasters frequently comment on the *appearance* of female athletes—their looks, grooming, demeanor—along with or instead of their athletic performance.

It's true that Harry Caray, one of our Cubs announcers, has been known to say things like, "He's a good-looking young man," but generally speaking, it is men's athletic abilities that sportscasters talk about, not how masculine they look or how attractive they are or aren't. That makes sense. And the same should hold true for female athletes. When a woman enters a sporting competition, she should be judged on how well she performs at that event—not on physical or social attributes that have no bearing on her athletic ability.

One effort we can make to begin correcting this sports reporting double standard is to write to the offending sportscasters and their employers when we hear or read sexist sports news. In a helpful tone, point out the inequities of reporting on men's and women's sports. You might also want to explain how such comments underplay the effects of years of practice and hard work, making it seem as though all you need to do to succeed in women's sports is to have a good complexion and look cute.

The other thing that absolutely has to happen for female athletes to be taken seriously is that we must first take ourselves seriously. Putting on lipstick in the middle of a tournament, as Marlene Piper did in 1968, will not help our cause! When was the last time you saw some guy in the dugout putting on mustache wax, or even combing his hair? If we're worrying about how we look in the middle of an inning, how can we possibly be concentrating on the game?

But it's deeper than these surface things. We also need to continue believing in ourselves, in our abilities, no matter how little reinforcement we get from the rest of the world. This means, for one thing, that we need to be as supportive as possible of women's teams of all kinds because a breakthrough in one sport makes an opening for women in every other sport. Such support can be as simple as attending games. In fact, game attendance is a critical factor in whether or not professional teams survive. As of 1988, there is only one women's professional sports league in existence: volleyball. If that league is going to exist, they will have to have fans in the stands. Of course, if women's teams aren't given media attention, no one knows when or where the games are, and, more often than not, no one even knows the teams exist. Which is exactly why media attention is so crucial.

In The News

Here's just one example of how women's sports typically fare in the news:

After the first Breeze game (Chicago's Major League Volleyball team), I anxiously awaited that evening's sportscast. Instead of footage of this incredibly fast-paced, breathtaking match between professionals, what I saw was extensive coverage of boys *high school* basketball scores. Apparently, professional women athletes are deemed less newsworthy than are adolescent schoolboys.

If asked, I'm sure most sports reporters would say they cover what their readers/viewers want to know about. I don't doubt that's true, but it's also true that the media can be very influential in shaping our views. If a few journalists got excited about women's sports and made them their cause célèbre, there is little doubt that they would be able to infect others with that enthusiasm. Perhaps as more women are able to crash the almost exclusively male club of sports reporting and gain the respect they deserve, we will get some help in this area. Until then, it's something of a vicious cycle: sporting events that draw large crowds are considered newsworthy, and in order to draw crowds the events need to be covered.

The media aren't the only ones responsible for getting the word out about women's sports, however. The sports organizations themselves need to promote. Between having little money (usually), and having to fight men's teams for space in the papers and for air time this is, I will grant, a difficult task. But sometimes the organizations themselves sabotage promotion of their teams. A case in point is women's Major League Volleyball. When the League was first announced at the end of 1986, I began working with their corporate headquarters in San Francisco, as well as with the manager of the local Chicago team on putting together an article—possibly several—to promote the team in *Windy City Times.* Everyone was very enthusiastic, very helpful, and very grateful for the publicity—until they discovered that *Windy City Times* is a gay and lesbian paper. I never heard another word from them. So strong is the fear of having female athletes be identified as lesbians, the PR folks were willing to forgo a source of free publicity—and to a potentially large percentage of their audience.

So far, I've been drawing my examples from volleyball, the only women's professional league currently in existence. The same problems of news coverage and promotion, however, were faced by the International Women's Professional Softball League during its all-too-brief existence—as well as by the three professional basketball leagues and by the professional football league, all of which have come and gone, in short order.

Clearly, getting coverage in the media is going to be a tall order. Men's professional baseball, basketball, and football are firmly entrenched in our cultural inheritance, and it won't be easy to squeeze ourselves into the hearts of sports fans, no matter how skilled we are. And unfortunately, given the odds we must fight to pursue athletics—unlike boys, who are motivated and guided through every stage of their athleticism—our skills aren't yet at the same level as men's. There are no quick solutions to these inequalities and problems, but there *are* solutions. We just need to begin applying ourselves: first, to finding the solutions, then to working on them in an organized fashion.

Coed Pro Sports?

The two main questions for women on the topic of coed pro sports are: Is that something that we really want? And even if it is, can we, in our wildest dreams, hope to get it?

The answer to the first question is a matter for each individual to decide as well as something women as a group must determine. And as with virtually everything in life, there are pros and cons to this issue—at both the individual and collective levels.

On the negative side, women will inevitably be compared harshly with their male counterparts. Any errors they make are bound to be attributed to their gender rather than to an off-day, a gap in training, or an isolated or individual weakness as it often is with men. Moreover, women are liable to be resented by many of their fellow players. There are also questions that can be raised about the ethics of certain practices in professional baseball concerning contracts, the trading of players, and so on. If the ethics of current baseball practices are, in fact, in question, do we want to buy into that system? Some feminists go so far as to question the whole ethic of sports competition—particularly the "winning is everything" type of philosophy. These are questions we must grapple with if we don't want to unthinkingly perpetuate immoral or unhealthy practices (or contribute to their perpetuation).[3] Also worth considering is what Dorothy Harris, a Penn State sports psychologist, has to say: " 'Why should women athletes be judged by the same standards we use for men?. . .Throughout sports we have different categories of competition.' A middleweight boxer like Sugar Ray Leonard, she points out, is not expected to be able to beat a heavyweight like Mike Tyson—yet both are called champions."[4]

On the other hand, there are numerous reasons why women might want to get involved in professional sports alongside men. While there would almost certainly be an initial negative response from male players and fans alike, in the long run, women ballplayers would be bound to earn respect (no matter how grudging)—a respect that will spill over into the other areas of life. After all, some of our greatest and most well-known heroes in this country are sports figures. (Ironically, of course, this very fact will make it that much harder for women to break into the sports domain, as men are often anxious to preserve the maleness of "hero-dom.") A side effect of the new-found respect we would gain might be a relaxation of the tension between men and women around issues of superiority, generally.

Beyond these social benefits, coed professional teams would yield very practical assistance to women's sports. Mainly, it is conceivable that this might be the only way for women ballplayers to get the opportunities, compensation, and attention they deserve. Because, as things stand now, women don't have either the power to control the media or the money to build a viable league—critical ingredients for success. If women were admitted as players to the major leagues, they would gain, over the years, the experience and respect needed to climb the ranks in baseball's power structure and work their way into positions of control. Doubtless, it would take time for women to accomplish this (as we've seen in the example of Blacks in the major leagues), but playing pro ball would at the very least ensure a ready-made audience—something our women's pro leagues unfortunately have thus far been unable to produce, much less guarantee.

So let's say you're convinced that coed professional baseball would have distinct advantages for women— gender-based cultural obstacles aside, are women *really* physically capable of playing professional sports beside men? Most of us know in our *bones*, the answer is yes. Fortuitously, for the sake of this argument, we have much more to go on than our female intuition. Indeed, I can offer support of three different types for these gut feelings: historical statements, current performance records, and scientific research.

In the realm of history, I submit as evidence former Cub Charlie Grimm's accolades for Dottie Schroeder of the All-American Girls Professional Baseball League and the minor league contract offer to Eleanor Engle of the AAGPBL.[5] Men's baseball was every bit as serious then, in the forties and fifties. And, especially in the days before expanded consciousness about women's abilities, it is unlikely that either the praises or the contract offer would have occurred if Schroeder and Engle were not genuinely capable.

As for actual current performance, one often hears that women aren't able to throw as well as men. Joan Joyce's record for throwing the fastest pitch in softball, which still holds, belies this assertion.[6] Furthermore, research confirms that the myth of women being unable to throw is exactly that: a myth. Studies by Anne Atwater of the

University of Arizona have led her to conclude that "women don't have any biomechanical problems with throwing. It's just that many women have never gotten beyond the childhood level of doing it."[7]

Records in other sports show that women's performances have closed gaps to within about ten percent of men's records in the last two decades.[8] And research by Kirk Cureton of the University of Georgia shows that given the same weight training, men and women will increase their muscle size by the same amount.[9]

Although most physiologists feel that differences in speed and strength will never disappear completely because of biologically different builds, and, therefore, women as a group may never surpass men as a group, it seems clear that some women will be faster and/or stronger than many men. Differences in ability already exist in pro ball clubs. Among the 1987 Cubs, for example, much has been made of right fielder Andre Dawson's comparatively superior arm strength. Also, it has often been pointed out that second baseman Ryne Sandberg or outfielder Bobby Dernier are faster on the basepaths than catcher Jody Davis.

So why would it be unreasonable to expect that women wouldn't fall into this same pattern of variance? It seems likely that some women would be faster than other players —male and female—and some would be slower. And in the area of arm strength, there is no reason, given proper training, why women couldn't be equally competitive. Again, if women receive the same opportunities and coaching from the beginning, there is nothing to prevent them (other than personal motivation and cultural barriers) from competing in professional baseball, or other sports for that matter.[10] Even if there were areas where male and female players would only blend well if some minor rules of play were changed, there are already precedents set for such types of change: equipment modifications over the years have resulted in revision of rules; strike zones have been known to shrink and grow; and the height of the pitcher's mound can increase and decrease. All things considered, it is primarily cultural obstructions that hold us back, mostly in the form of incredibly confining definitions for masculinity and femininity.

The Language Trap

When we give a name to something, that name becomes our reality. Once we assign a label and describe or define that something, the label and the definition become proof of one another in circular fashion.

If we take the name *chair*, for example, and describe it as "a seat, especially for one person, usually having four legs for support and a rest for the back"; and if I then point to the scaly creature with fins and gills in my aquarium and tell you it's a chair, you can cite our definition of *chair* and tell me I'm wrong. Yet a chair is only a chair because that's what we've decided to call it—we could just as easily have called "a seat . . . having four legs for support and a rest for the back" a *fish*. As Jane Wagner and Lily Tomlin's creation Trudy says, "What is reality anyway? Nothin' but a collective hunch."[11]

Though this may seem like little more than an interesting mental and verbal exercise, when applied to the words *masculine* and *feminine,* the relationship between words and their definitions have very real consequences in our lives. It's as if because someone, somewhere along the line, decided that x, y, and z behaviors would be called masculine, and a, b, and c behaviors would be called feminine, that's reality. We could just as easily have said that a, b, and c behaviors would be called masculine and x, y, and z would be feminine behaviors. Some behaviors, of course, are related to biological features and are therefore sex-differentiated. But most behaviors are learned, and as such are a matter of our "collective hunch"—a question of how "we" decided to define them. Because of such an often arbitrary assignment of certain behaviors to men and others to women, we have to choose between accepting so-called reality and being told that we are abnormal or, at the very least, that we are wrong to suggest another definition.

Many behaviors—both those that have been accepted as male and those that are thought of as female—are not necessarily either good or bad, nor should any of these traits be more enviable than any other. The only thing that makes feminine behaviors less than desirable is that such characteristics are automatically assigned to us regardless of our own unique temperament and personality. It is this arbitrariness that makes femininity constraining. As it turns out, of course, the definitions of masculine and feminine have also generally worked to the advantage of men. Men may not have consciously conspired against women in formulating these definitions, but the fact remains that because men benefit from this reality in many ways, they have a stake in preserving it.

One of the tools they have to ensure that women don't stray too far also has to do with language. "Since there are very real and severe consequences of being Lesbian, the word itself is a powerful threat and is often used as a weapon. It seems to surface most often when men feel threatened by girls and women acting outside the bounds of traditional sex-stereotyped roles"[12]—like with team sports.

Given that this weapon looms large and powerful over women's sports—effectively dissuading many women from pursuing athletics and discrediting those that do—defusing the language of gender becomes critical. Since the Women's Movement of the seventies, clear progress has been made along these lines; definitions of appropriate masculine and appropriate feminine behaviors have loosened up considerably. And the Stonewall resistance of 1969 has even removed some of the stigma attached to being gay or lesbian. But as anyone who has had to grapple with being labeled *butch* or *femme*, or who has had *lezzie* or *fuckin' dyke* thrown derisively at her ought to know, we have a long way to go yet. Our progress of the last decade or two, however, indicates that there is reason to hope. Persistence is the key. After all, we just have to redefine a few words!

The Future Of Dyke Softball

Whatever happens with women's sports—whether we revive women's pro baseball, play alongside the men, or never play professionally—one thing seems to be a safe bet: somewhere, everywhere, across the country, there *will* be lesbians playing softball. And that's as it should be. While it is terribly important for women athletes to be recognized in professional sports, not all of us, now or ever, will be able to or will want to go that route. For us, there still needs to be dyke softball, in the way that recreational softball and baseball exist now for men not in pro sports. The physical and social benefits of softball should be accessible to everyone.

Also, though it is to be hoped that people will become enlightened enough ultimately to discard their homophobia, those changes aren't going to happen any time soon. In the meantime, softball will remain, as it has been for over half a century, an invaluable meeting ground and a source of validation for lesbians. There will always be lesbians who are more at home in softball than in a bar or at a cultural event or political rally. For them, dyke softball is an essential connection to the community. Even for those of us who are active in several spheres, softball provides things we don't get elsewhere, including a constructive way to dissipate our tensions, as well as a unique environment for forming friendships. It is because of benefits like the latter that it seems probable, even in some mythical homophobia-free world, that softball would continue much as it has in the lesbian community.

But do we want to keep it exactly as it is? Or do we want to mold it to suit our needs even better? The last question is admittedly tricky in that we all have different needs and different conceptions of what will make it better. Nevertheless, some suggestions seem in order here.

First, more teams need to rethink competition from a feminist perspective. There are those who see all and any competition as inherently bad. Whether that's true as competition is now constructed, or not, it doesn't have to be that way. Competition is a negative experience when much more emphasis is placed on the final outcome than on the process—as if only the last inning counts, with its final score. When that happens, we neglect all of the individual moments that got us there—moments of challenge, breathtaking grace and skill, triumph, exhilaration, and, yes, even the errors, which have their pluses when viewed constructively.

Most of us grew up believing that winning is intrinsically valuable and so have taken for granted that proving one's superiority over someone is something to strive for. I don't think there's anything wrong with winning per se, but trying to assert one's superiority does not seem at all humanist, much less feminist. What makes much more sense is striving for one's own personal best—striving, simply, to play well. Then, winning is nothing more than a superfluous extra. In fact, it may be that the only good

reasons to play well are to have fun and for personal satisfaction and because not playing well can be a frustrating
experience.

When too much importance is placed on winning, it not
only can detract from our fun, but it may also keep some
women from playing, feeling they aren't good enough to
participate. For these two reasons, and perhaps others, we
should seriously consider whether we want to accept current conventions surrounding competition or whether we
want to devalue the class-like hierarchy of winner/loser.

What would also improve dyke softball is better overall
integration: racially as well as with other parts of the community, including the literary/political women and, on a
limited basis, the gay male population. (Limited, in the
latter case, because women-only space is critical for bonding—which is just as important among women as among
men—and, in this male-dominated society, women-only
settings are also invaluable for creating psychic space.)
The value of greater integration has to do with softball's
unifying quality: if dyke softball teams were more racially
mixed and more intertwined with other parts of the community, the community as a whole would be that much
stronger and more of a force to be reckoned with.

These are but a couple of considerations that need to
be made if dyke softball is to be an even better institution
than it already is in our community. No doubt there are
other ways in which it might be improved. And thinking
and talking about these improvements is one way of keeping softball vital. That, after all, is *the* most essential thing:
keeping dyke softball alive. Because for me, and for many
other lesbians, home plate is where the heart is, and where
the heart is, that's home.

Notes

1. Ruth Bennett, quoted in Betty Hicks, "Lesbian Athletes," *Christopher Street* 4, no. 3 (October/November 1979): 42-50.

2. "The Form Is Big League: Gals Go All Out in Finale of Softball Tournament," *New York Sunday News*, October 13, 1968, pp. 4-5.

3. A good place to start if you're looking for a feminist analysis of sports is Mary A. Boutilier and Lucinda SanGiovanni, *The Sporting Woman* (Champaign, Ill.: Human Kinetics Publishers, 1983).

4. William F. Allman, "Ms. Conceptions: The Female Athlete," *Hippocrates* 2, no. 1 (January/February 1988): 93.

5. See chap. 2 for more on this. See also Sharon Taylor-Roepke, "The Other Major League" (paper delivered at the North American Society for Sports History, May 25, 1981); Sharon Roepke, *Diamond Gals* (Marcellus, Mich.: A.A.G.B.L. Cards, 1986); and Jay Feldman, "Perspective," *Sports Illustrated*, June 10, 1985).

6. See Jonathan Ullyot, "Where the Women Are," *Women's Sports and Fitness* 9, no. 6 (June 1987): 56; and chap. 2 of *Diamonds Are A Dyke's Best Friend* for details of this record.

7. Allman, p. 93.

8. Ibid.; Ullyot.

9. Allman, p. 92.

10. However, something like football—where physical size can be a major factor—might be out of the question for most.

11. Jane Wagner, *The Search for Signs of Intelligent Life in the Universe* (New York: Harper & Row, 1986), p. 18.

12. Joan C. Gondola and Toni Fitzpatrick, "Homophobia in Girls' Sports: 'Names' That Can Hurt Us . . . ALL of Us," *Equal Play* (Spring/Summer 1985), pp. 18-19.

Appendix A

Who's Represented Here, Anyway?

While this book is not, as I have said, any sort of serious sociological study, I think it is not only useful but interesting as well to get a sense of who is represented here. Consequently, I have put together some very basic figures about the sixty-five women who I talked to or who wrote to me about *Diamonds Are A Dyke's Best Friend*. (An asterisk [*] indicates that the information in question was not provided by all sixty-five women.)

Age range*: 23-52
Average age: 33.6
Most common age: 32 (6 women)
Level of education:*

high school degree	4
technical training and/or some college	13
four-year degree	17
masters's degree	10
doctorate degree	3
specialized degree[1]	2

Ethnic background:[2]

White	44 (68%)
Black	4 (6%)
Hispanic	6 (9%)
Asian	5 (8%)
Jewish	4 (6%)
Native American	2 (3%)

A sampling of occupations:

accounting manager, attorney, bartender, bookseller, carpenter, clerk, computer programmer, drug counselor, environmental engineer, film animator, folk singer, nurse's aide, paralegal, park maintenance, photographer, photo lab technician, printer, professor, publisher, reporter, research scientist, social worker, teacher, typesetter, veterinarian, and writer.

Notes

1. One juris, one veterinary medicine.

2. To put these numbers on ethnicity in perspective, I called the U.S. Bureau of the Census (December 30, 1987) for comparable figures for the United States as a whole. Based on 1986 census figures, the percentages are as follows: White, 85%; Black, 12%; Hispanic, 7%; and "other," 3%.

Appendix B

Where Do They Come From?

The women represented in this book are from the east coast, the west coast, the South, the Southwest, and the Midwest. More specifically: California (15), Florida (3), Georgia (2), Illinois (23), Kentucky (1), Massachusetts (1), New Mexico (2), New York (4), South Dakota (3), Tennessee (2), Texas (2), Washington D.C. (3), and Wisconsin (3).[1] The women whom I have directly quoted in these pages are listed below, in alphabetical order, with the cities and states where they live and the chapters in which they appear.

Name	Chapters	Where She's From
Miki Adachi	4, 5, 8	Foster City, California
Toni Armstrong, Jr.	7	Chicago, Illinois
Mary Azzano	9	Chicago, Illinois
Bea	3, 7, 8	Washington, D.C.
Susan Begg	3, 6, 8, 9	Ithaca, New York
Joan Bender	5, 8	Rapid City, South Dakota
Beth	6, 8	Los Angeles, California

B. Victoria	4	Tampa, Florida
Nancy C.	6	Evanston, Illinois
Carrie	9	Chicago, Illinois
Cathy	3	Chicago, Illinois
Jean Claiborne	7, 8	Nashville, Tennessee
Connie	3	El Paso, Texas
Rhonda Craven	3, 7, 8	Chicago, Illinois
Alix Dobkin	4, 5, 6	Woodstock, New York
Ellen	3	Ithaca, New York
Erin	5	Chicago, Illinois
Mary Farmer	4, 7, 8, 9	Washington, D.C.
Florence	5, 7, 8	San Diego, California
Fran	3, 4, 9	Clearwater, Florida
Barbara Grier	2, 7, 8, 9	Tallahassee, Florida
Pat Griffin	4, 6, 7	Belchertown, Massachusetts
Gyacko	6	Los Angeles, California
Ellen Heimbuck	3, 7	Vermillion, South Dakota
Louise Hernandez	3, 4	Poway, California
Janice Hughes	3	Washington, D.C.
Jody	5	Evanston, Illinois
J. T.	3, 5, 6	Evanston, Illinois
Laurie	3, 4, 7, 8	S. Suburban Chicago, Illinois
Liz	3, 7	Albuquerque, New Mexico
Linda Locke	4, 5, 8, 9	Berkeley, California
M.	4	West Allis, Wisconsin
Mei	Intro., 7, 8, 9	Berkeley, California
Celeste Methot	5, 7, 9	Nashville, Tennessee
Mo	5, 7	Chicago, Illinois
Meryl Moskowitz	3, 4, 8	Los Angeles, California
Missy Myers	3, 5, 7, 9	Chicago, Illinois
Achy Obejas	6, 7	Chicago, Illinois
Nan O'Connor	9	San Francisco, California
Olivia	3, 4, 5, 8	Berkeley, California
Pat Parker	3, 5, 7, 8	Walnut Creek, California
Kathy Phillips	3, 6	San Francisco, California

P. L.	5, 7	Chicago, Illinois
Polly	6, 7	Los Angeles, California
R. J.	4, 6, 7, 8	South Dakota
Paula Sanchez	6	Chicago, Illinois
Melinda B. Shaw	3, 7, 8	Ithaca, New York
She-Her	3, 7	Chicago, Illinois
Starla Sholl	4, 8	Chicago, Illinois
Spike	8	Chicago, Illinois
Stephie	5, 6, 7, 8, 9	Chicago, Illinois
Suzi	6, 8	Milwaukee, Wisconsin
Judy Thompson	5, 8, 9	San Diego, California
V.	3, 8	Chicago, Illinois
Glenna M. Voigt	3	Albuquerque, New Mexico

Notes

1. In addition, numerous other geographical areas (including Canada) are represented via material quoted from printed sources.

Bibliography

Allman, William F. "Ms. Conceptions: The Female Athlete." *Hippocrates* 2, no. 1 (January/February 1988): 92-93.

"Amazons to Meet Ms. Fitz's." *Lesbian Tide* 6, no. 6 (May/June 1977): 33.

Baker, William J. *Sports in the Western World.* Totowa, N.J.: Rowman & Littlefield, 1982.

B. G. "Hialeah Sandettes Edge All-Stars." *Lesbian Tide* 3, no. 3 (October 1973): 22.

"Bloomer Ball Tossers: Were Pinched and Raised a Rough House in Texas Jail." *Cincinnati Enquirer,* July 20, 1903.

Boutilier, Mary A., and Lucinda SanGiovanni. *The Sporting Woman.* Champaign, Ill.: Human Kinetics Publishers, 1983.

Brickell, Beth (writer, producer, and director). *Summer's End.* Los Angeles, 1986. Film. Distributed on videotape by Direct Cinema Ltd., Los Angeles.

Brown, Rita Mae. "Take a Lesbian to Lunch" and "Conclusion." In her *A Plain Brown Rapper.* Oakland, Calif.: Diana Press, 1976.

Butt, Dorcas Susan. *Psychology of Sport: The Behavior, Motivation, Personality, and Performance of Athletes.* New York: Van Nostrand Reinhold Co., 1976.

Clinton, Kate. "Making Light: Notes on Feminist Humor." *Trivia: A Journal of Ideas,* vol. 1 (Fall 1982).

Cobhan, Linn ni. "Lesbians in Physical Education and Sport." In *Lesbian Studies: Present and Future,* edited by Margaret Cruikshank. Old Westbury, N.Y.: Feminist Press, 1982.

Collins, Dottie. "Cooperstown 1989." *All American Girls Professional Baseball League Newsletter,* April 1987.

Cooney, Ellen. *All the Way Home.* New York: G. P. Putnam's Sons, 1984.

DeCosta, Lou. "Pro Softball's New Pitch." *womenSports* (June 1977), pp. 35-38.

"A Diamond These Girls' Best Friend." *Daily Star*, September 18, 1984.

Edwards, Harry. "Desegregating Sport." In *Out of the Bleachers: Writings on Women and Sport*, edited by Stephanie L. Twin. Old Westbury, N.Y.: Feminist Press, 1979.

Edwards, Valerie. "Notso Amazons Not So Competitive Softball," in *Everywoman's Almanac 1987*. Toronto, 1987.

Ehrenreich, Barbara, and Deirdre English. *Complaints and Disorders: The Sexual Politics of Sickness*. Old Westbury, N.Y.: Feminist Press, 1973.

Fasteau, Brenda Feigen. "Giving Women a Sporting Chance." In *Out of the Bleachers: Writings on Women and Sport*, edited by Stephanie L. Twin. Old Westbury, N.Y.: Feminist Press, 1979.

Feldman, Jay. "Perspective." *Sports Illustrated* (June 10, 1985).

Fidler, Merrie A. "The Establishment of Softball as a Sport for American Women, 1900-1940." In *Her Story in Sport*, edited by Reet Howell. West Point, N.Y.: Leisure Press, 1982.

Figel, Bill. "Absence of Coaches Hurts Women's Sports." *Chicago Sun-Times*, June 16, 1986.

Figel, Bill. "Hustle Coach: Lesbianism Factor on Team." *Chicago Sun-Times*, June 16, 1986.

Figel, Bill. "Lesbians in the World of Athletics." *Chicago Sun-Times*, June 16, 1986.

Figel, Bill. "NU's Single Has a Cautious View." *Chicago Sun-Times*, June 16, 1986.

"The Form Is Big League: Gals Go All Out in Finale of Softball Tournament." *New York Sunday News*, October 13, 1968, pp. 4-5.

Frommer, Harvey. *Sports Roots*. New York: Atheneum, 1979.

Gerber, Ellen W., et al. *The American Woman in Sport*. Reading, Mass.: Addison-Wesley, 1974.

Gondola, Joan C. and Toni Fitzpatrick. "Homophobia in Girls' Sports: 'Names' That Can Hurt Us . . . ALL of Us." *Equal Play* (Spring/Summer 1985).

Gorov, Lynda. "Parks Shutting Us Out, Women Softballers Say." *Chicago Sun-Times*, April 9, 1987.

Greene, Pat. "Beautiful Women's Softball." *Lesbian Tide* 2, no. 12 (July 1973): 3.

Gregorich, Barbara. *She's On First*. Chicago: Contemporary Books, 1987.

Guttmann, Allen. "Women's Sports." In his *A Whole New Ball Game: An Interpretation of American Sports*. Chapel Hill: University of North Carolina Press, 1988.

Halpert, Felicia E. "Heros Wanted: Celebrating Women's Team Sports Will Encourage Girls to Take the Field." *Ms.* (March 1988), pp. 84-85.

Halpert, Felicia E. "How the Game Was Invented." *Women's Sports and Fitness* 9, no. 7 (July 1987): 34.

Hart, Marie M. "On Being Female in Sport." In *Out of the Bleachers: Writings on Women and Sport*, edited by Stephanie L. Twin. Old Westbury, N.Y.: Feminist Press, 1979.

Hayden, Sandy. "Giving Her Away." *Focus* (May/June 1980).

Hibben, Maryhel. "Dyke Softball." *Leaping Lesbian* (May 1977).

Hicks, Betty. "Lesbian Athletics." *Christopher Street* 4, no. 3 (October/November 1979).

Hogan, Candace Lyle. "Diamonds and Dust." *Women's Sports* (June 1976).

Hogan, Candace Lyle. "What's the Future for Women's Sports?" *Women's Sports and Fitness* 9, no. 6 (June 1987).

Janisis, and Laurie Bach. "Diamonds Are A Dyke's Best Friend." *Lesbian Tide* 6, no. 6 (May/June 1977).

Johanek, Linda. "Sports Seen: Softball Scores with Area Women." *Today's Chicago Woman*, August 1986.

Kaplan, Janice. *Women and Sports*. New York: Viking Press, 1979.

Kazin, Michael. "Hottest Baseball in the Bay." *Berkeley Barb*, June 21-July 4, 1979.

Kidd, Dorothy. "Dyke Dynamos: Women in Sports." *Pink Ink* (Toronto) (August 1983).

Knudson, R. R. *Zanboomer*. New York: Dell Publishing, 1978.

Kohn, Alfie. "It's Hard to Get Left Out of a Pair." *Psychology Today* (October 1987), p. 54.

Kort, Michele. "Body Politics." *Chrysalis*, vol. 7 (1979).

Kort, Michele. "Faster Than a Speeding Bullet." *Ms.* 16, no. 5 (November 1987): 90.

Kort, Michele. "High Marks for Homophobia." *Women's Sports* (November 1982).

Kort, Michele. "*Ms.* Conversation," *Ms.* (February 1988), pp. 58-62.

Koslow, Sally Platkin. "Why Do Women Want to Be Jocks?" *Mademoiselle*, vol. 87 (August 1975).

"LALALA Revisited!" *Lesbian Tide* 6, no. 6 (May/June 1977).

Lenskyj, Helen. *Out of Bounds: Women, Sport and Sexuality*. Toronto: Women's Press, 1986.

"Lesbians Strike Out at Softball Camp." *Lesbian Connection* (1977).

Markel, Robert; Nancy Brooks; and Susan Markel. "Softball." In their *For the Record: Women in Sports*. New York: World Almanac Publishers, 1985.

McLaughlin, Patricia. "Diamond Duds: There's No Uniform Opinion on Why Softball Wears Well." *Chicago Tribune*, May 15, 1988.

McNaron, Toni. "An Interview with the Wilder Ones." *So's Your Old Lady*, no. 10 (September 1975).

Miller Lite Report on Women in Sports. New York: Women's Sports Foundation, 1985.

Morris, Bonnie J. "The Amazon Skills Curriculum." *Hot Wire: A Journal of Women's Music and Culture* 4, no. 1 (November 1987): 37.

Murphy, Patricia J. "Sport and Gender." In Wilbert Marcellus Leonard II, *A Sociological Perspective of Sport*, 2d ed. Minneapolis, Minn.: Burgess Publishing, 1984.

Nelson, Mariah Burton. Foreword in *More Golden Apples*, edited by Sandra Martz. Manhattan Beach, Calif.: Papier-Mache Press, 1986.

Nelson, Mariah Burton. "My Mother, My Rival." *Ms.* (May 1988), pp. 88-89.

Nevius, C. W. "Theories on Homosexuality in Sports." *San Francisco Chronicle*, May 14, 1981.

Oberlander, Susan. "After Eight Years, Female Athletes' Suit against Temple U. Goes to Trial in U.S. District Court This Week." *Chronicle of Higher Education* (March 30, 1988).

Oglesby, Carole A., ed. *Women and Sport: From Myth to Reality.* Philadelphia: Lea & Febiger, 1978.

Phibbs, Chris. "Political Sweat." *Broadside* 6 (Toronto) (July 1985), p. 5.

Pogrebin, Letty Cottin. *Among Friends.* New York: McGraw-Hill Book Co., 1987.

"Power of Title IX Restored." *Headway: The Women's Sports Foundation Newsletter* (Spring 1988).

Roepke, Sharon L. *Diamond Gals.* Marcellus, Mich.: A.A.G.B.L. Cards, 1986.

Rossellini, Lynn. "Homosexuals in Sports: Lesbians and Straights." *New York Post*, December 13, 1975.

Rover, Rhoda. "Softball: Slow Pitch, Hard Core." *Lesbian Tide* 6, no. 2 (September/October 1976): 6-7, 37.

"Sandettes Blast Tide." *Lesbian Tide* 3, no. 4 (November 1973): 23-25.

Schoenstein, Ralph. *Diamonds For Lori and Me: A Father, A Daughter and Baseball.* New York: Beech Tree Books, 1988.

Sherriff, M. C. "The Status of Female Athletes as Viewed by Selected Peers and Parents in Certain High Schools of Central California." Master's thesis, Chico State College, 1969. Quoted in Ellen W. Gerber et al., *The American Woman in Sport.* Reading, Mass.: Addison-Wesley, 1974.

Skeen, Anita. "City Park: March Sunday." In her *Each Hand a Map.* Tallahassee, Fla.: Naiad Press, 1986, pp. 71-72.

"Soapbox." (Letters to ed.) *Hot Wire: A Journal of Women's Music and Culture* 4, no. 1 (November 1987): 7.

Sports Illustrated Sports Poll '86. New York: Time, Inc., 1986.

Stanek, Carolyn. *The Complete Guide to Women's College Athletics*. Chicago: Contemporary Books, 1981.

Stackel, Leslie. "Old-Timers' Day for Some 'All-American Girls.' " *Ms.* (October 1982), p. 20.

Stevenson, Louise L. "Sarah Porter Educates Useful Ladies, 1847-1900." *Winterthur Portfolio* 18, no. 1 (Spring 1983): 39-59.

Swallow, Jean. *Leave A Light On For Me*. San Francisco: Spinsters/Aunt Lute, 1986.

Talamini, John T., and Charles H. Page, eds. *Sport and Society: An Anthology*. Boston: Little, Brown & Co., 1973.

Taylor, Janis L. (director and producer). *When Diamonds Were a Girl's Best Friend: The 1986 Reunion of the All-American Girls Baseball League*. Chicago: 1987. Video documentary.

Taylor-Roepke, Sharon. "The Other Major League." Paper delivered at the North American Society for Sports History, May 25, 1981.

Twin, Stephanie L. "Jock and Jill: Aspects of Women's Sports History in America, 1870-1940." Ph.D. thesis, Rutgers University, 1978.

Twin, Stephanie L., ed. *Out of the Bleachers: Writings on Women and Sport*. Old Westbury, N.Y.: Feminist Press, 1979.

Tyson, Molly. "No Joy in Mudville." *womenSports*, vol. 4 (January 1977), pp. 48-52.

Ullyot, Jonathan, comp. "Where the Women Are." *Women's Sports and Fitness* 9, no. 6 (June 1987): 56.

Vogan, Sara. *In Shelly's Leg*. St. Paul, Minn.: Graywolf Press, 1985.

"We Have to Be Our Own Spark: Interview with 'Gente' Third-World Lesbian Softball Team." *Lesbian Tide* 3, no. 11 (July 1974): 6-7, 25-28.

Weiss, Paul. "Women Athletes." In *Sport and Society: An Anthology*, edited by John T. Talamini and Charles H. Page. Boston: Little, Brown & Co., 1973.

Young, David. "Seasons in the Sun." *Women's Sports* (October 1982), pp. 48-52, 72, 74.

Zipter, Yvonne. "Making Conversation with Kate Clinton." *Hot Wire: A Journal of Women's Music and Culture* 1, no. 1 (November 1984).

Zolna, Ed, and Mike Conklin. *Mastering Softball*. Chicago: Contemporary Books, 1981.

Other titles from Firebrand Books include:

A Burst of Light, Essays by Audre Lorde/$7.95

Dykes To Watch Out For, Cartoons by Alison Bechdel/$6.95

The Fires Of Bride, A Novel by Ellen Galford/$8.95

Getting Home Alive by Aurora Levins Morales and Rosario Morales/$8.95

Good Enough To Eat, A Novel by Lesléa Newman/$8.95

Jonestown & Other Madness, Poetry by Pat Parker/$5.95

The Land Of Look Behind, Prose and Poetry by Michelle Cliff/$6.95

A Letter To Harvey Milk, Short Stories by Lesléa Newman/$8.95

Living As A Lesbian, Poetry by Cheryl Clarke/$6.95

Making It, A Woman's Guide to Sex in the Age of AIDS by Cindy Patton and Janis Kelly/$3.95

Mohawk Trail by Beth Brant (*Degonwadonti*)/$6.95

Moll Cutpurse, A Novel by Ellen Galford/$7.95

More Dykes To Watch Out For, Cartoons by Alison Bechdel/$7.95

The Monarchs Are Flying, A Novel by Marion Foster/$8.95

My Mama's Dead Squirrel, Lesbian Essays on Southern Culture by Mab Segrest/$8.95

Politics Of The Heart, A Lesbian Parenting Anthology edited by Sandra Pollack and Jeanne Vaughn/$11.95

Presenting. . .Sister Noblues by Hattie Gossett/$8.95

A Restricted Country by Joan Nestle/$8.95

Sanctuary, A Journey by Judith McDaniel/$7.95

Shoulders, A Novel by Georgia Cotrell/$8.95

The Sun Is Not Merciful, Short Stories by Anna Lee Walters/$7.95

Tender Warriors, A Novel by Rachel Guido deVries/$7.95

This Is About Incest by Margaret Randall/$7.95

The Threshing Floor, Short Stories by Barbara Burford/$7.95

Trash, Stories by Dorothy Allison/$8.95

The Women Who Hate Me, Poetry by Dorothy Allison/$5.95

Words To The Wise, A Writer's Guide to Feminist and Lesbian Periodicals & Publishers by Andrea Fleck Clardy/$3.95

Yours In Struggle, Three Feminist Perspectives on Anti-Semitism and Racism by Elly Bulkin, Minnie Bruce Pratt, and Barbara Smith/$8.95

You can buy Firebrand titles at your bookstore, or order them directly from the publisher (141 The Commons, Ithaca, New York 14850, 607-272-0000).

Please include $1.75 shipping for the first book and $.50 for each additional book.

A free catalog is available on request.